KELEC

GH00832245

THE
TRUTHS
OF LIFE

May you bo Empowered to Excel

The Mysteries of Dreams & Visions

DR. JOHN OWUSU-ANSAH

Published by
DR. JOHN OWUSU-ANSAH

LIVING WORD TEMPLE
Tottenham Branch
2 Chapel Place, 6 White Hart Lane,
Tottenham, London N17 8DP

Tel: +44 (0) 208 801 7885,
Fax: +44 (0) 208 885 4045,

Email: drjohn@livingwordtemple.org
www.livingwordtemple.org

Layout & Print in the UK at supremeprinters.com

ACKNOWLEDGMENT

I would like first of all to thank the Lord Jesus Christ who has called me into His church to serve His flock. I see this as a great honour to serve the people of the Living God.

My special thanks also go to my wife Cecilia and daughter Joy Evangel who have specifically honoured the Lord to give me time to write this insightful book of deliverance for God's people. Moreover , my sincere gratitude go to my Secretary Ms. Daphne Namigadde who took much time to put the Manuscript together and my Administrator Elder Kwadwo Fordwuor who organised the editing and production of the manuscript. And finally all members of Living Word Temple in London who forcefully supported me in prayer.

May the Almighty God continue to bless you abundantly.

INTRODUCTION

This book is a special gift from God to all humanity; God has a supernatural plan for every man. He has power to make and transform lives. He has created us to understand His ways and actions. This great God uses symbols to speak and direct us to achievement or warn us of our ways, actions and behaviours.

This book is a mystery of solid biblical based interpretation with over 332 symbols and over 561 scriptures. It has not been complied by mere intents of man's heart or mind rather the endowerment and inspiration of the Holy Spirit's insight to benefit the reader.

This is an insight of hidden truths of life and discovery of God's plan to reveal every satanic schemes and hindrances in the path way of blessings and enlightment to your destiny.

The Lord Jesus Christ spoke many parables and proverbs to His disciples then explained later in plain words and He continues to speak today.

I thank my God that He has given me an insightful revelation about His plan through symbols, visions and dreams. My dear friend, this small book is a master piece to guide you in understanding your dreams and visions empowered by the Lord Jesus Christ. As you read this book, may the presence of God fill your heart to activate His power for your freedom.

May the Lord richly bless you.

HOW TO USE THIS BOOK

This book has been arranged in alphabetical order from A-Z for easy access and reading, page one of this book has listing of symbols beginning from A then continues in that order.

If you don't find the corresponding word or symbol you saw in your dream or don't understand any part of the book, do not be worried, just go to the last page for my contacts, you can email me or call the number and by the grace of God, I will be empowered to explain it clearly to you. May the most high God empower you and stay blessed.

A

AN ANTELOPE CAUGHT IN A NET
Is a figure of one exhausted with in effectual attempt to release himself.

ISAIAH 51:20
Your sons have fainted; they lie at the head of all the streets, like an antelope in a net; they are full of the wrath of the Lord, the rebuke of your God.

AN ANTELOPE IN A NET
This represents unavoidable vengeance of God.

LAMENTATIONS 1:13
From on high he sent fire, sent it down into my bones. He spread a net for my feet and turned me back. He made me desolate, faint all the day long.

EZEKIEL 12:13
I will spread my net for him, and he will be caught in my snare; I will bring him to Babylonia, the land of the Chaldeans, but he will not see it, and there he will die.

HOSEA 7:12
When they go, I will throw my net over them; I will pull them down like the birds in the sky. When I hear them flocking together, I will catch them.

ANOINTING OIL
Is endowerment of power with the spirit of God

1 JOHN 2:20
But you have an anointing from the Holy One, and all of you know the truth

ANT
Weak but has wisdom and foresight or an organised army.

PROVERBS 6:6
Go to the ant, you sluggard; consider its ways and be wise.

PROVERBS 30:25
Ants are creatures of little strength, yet they store up their food in the summer;

ASHES
A sign of mourning

JOB 2:8
Then Job took a piece of broken pottery and scraped himself with it as he sat among the ashes.

ISAIAH 58:5
Is this the kind of fast I have chosen, only a day for people to humble themselves? Is it only for bowing one's head like a reed and for lying in sackcloth and ashes? Is that what you call a fast, a day acceptable to the LORD?

BRIGHT STAR
Represents Christ.

REVELATION 22:16
"I, Jesus, have sent my angel to give you this testimony for the churches. I am the Root and the Offspring of David, and the bright Morning Star."

BURNING MOUNTIAN
Signifies destroying enemies.

JEREMIAH 51:25
I am against you, you destroying mountain, you who destroy the whole earth," declares the LORD. "I will stretch out my hand against you, roll you off the cliffs, and make you a burned-out mountain.

BAKING IN INTENSE HEAT
Speedy destruction.

HOSEA 7:4, 6-7
4 They are all adulterers, burning like an oven whose fire the baker need not stir from the kneading of the dough till it rises.
6 Their hearts are like an oven; they approach him with intrigue. Their passion smolders all night; in the morning it blazes like a flaming fire.
7 All of them are hot as an oven;
they devour their rulers. All their kings fall, and none of them calls on me.

BALDNESS
Without anointing.

2 KINGS 2:23
From there Elisha went up to Bethel. As he was walking along the road, some youths came out of the town and jeered at him. "Go on up, you baldhead!" they said. "Go on up, you baldhead!"

BANNER
Is an indication of a memorial.

EXODUS 17:15
Moses built an altar and called it the LORD is my Banner

BAT
Destruction coming upon fruit bearing.

ISAIAH 2:19 - 21
19 In that day there will be an altar to the LORD in the heart of Egypt, and a monument to the LORD at its border.
20 It will be a sign and witness to the LORD Almighty in the land of Egypt. When they cry out to the LORD because of their oppressors, he will send them a saviour and defender, and he will rescue them.

21 *So the LORD will make himself known to the Egyptians, and in that day they will acknowledge the LORD. They will worship with sacrifices and grain offerings; they will make vows to the LORD and keep them.*

BEAR
Sign of the anti Christ.

A bear ate up the forty two who were laughing at Elisha as a bald headed man and David also killed a bear after taking one of his sheep.

2 KINGS 2:23-24

23 *From there Elisha went up to Bethel. As he was walking along the road, some boys came out of the town and jeered at him. "Get out of here, baldy!" they said. "Get out of here, baldy!"*
24 *He turned around, looked at them and called down a curse on them in the name of the LORD. Then two bears came out of the woods and mauled forty-two of the boys.*

1 SAMUEL 17:36

36 *Your servant has killed both the lion and the bear; this uncircumcised Philistine will be like one of them, because he has defied the armies of the living God.*

BEAST
The figurative is sensual, grovelling ferocious and brutal nature of men

Also means enemies. So seeing a beast in visions and dreams refers to the flesh.

Your ability or thinking is controlled by the flesh or to walk in the flesh.

Having fleshly desires instead of spiritual embodiments or falling in the hands of brutal men or escaping from the hands of brutal men depending the nature of the vision

PSALMS 73:22

I was senseless and ignorant; I was a brute beast before you.

1 CORINTHIANS 15:32

If I fought wild beasts in Ephesus with no more than human hopes, what have I gained? If the dead are not raised, "Let us eat and drink, for tomorrow we die."

ACTS 19:29

Soon the whole city was in an uproar. The people seized Gaius and Aristarchus, Paul's travelling companions from Macedonia, and all of them rushed together into the theatre.

BEES
Meaning - Interferences and resentment

PSALMS 118:12
They swarmed around me like bees, but they were consumed as quickly as burning thorns; in the name of the LORD I cut them down.

DEUTERONOMY 1:44
The Amorites who lived in those hills came out against you; they chased you like a swarm of bees and beat you down from Seir all the way to Hormah

BEING UNDER WATER
Is a figure of destruction.

MATTHEW 11:23
And you, Capernaum, will you be lifted up to the skies? No, you will go down to the depths. If the miracles that were performed in you had been performed in Sodom, it would have remained to this day.

REVELATION 1:17
When I saw him, I fell at his feet as though dead. Then he placed his right hand on me and said: "Do not be afraid. I am the First and the Last

BINDING OF ROPES
Is a sign of absolute surrender

JUDGES 16:11-12
11 *He said, "If anyone ties me securely with new ropes that have never been used, I'll become as weak as any other man."*
12 *So Delilah took new ropes and tied him with them. Then, with men hidden in the room, she called to him, "Samson, the Philistines are upon you!" But he snapped the ropes off his arms as if they were threads.*

2 SAMUEL 17:13
If he withdraws into a city, then all Israel will bring ropes to that city, and we will drag it down to the valley until not so much as a pebble is left."

BITTING YOURSELF
Taking your life in your own hands.

JOB 13:14
Why do I put myself in jeopardy and take my life in my hands?

C

CATTLE / COW
Meaning - Possession or proud wealthy rulers.

AMOS 4:1
Hear this word, you cows of Bashan on Mount Samaria, you women who oppress the poor and crush the needy and say to your husbands, "Bring us some drinks!"

GENESIS 41:2
When out of the river there came up seven cows, sleek and fat, and they grazed among the reeds.

CHAMBER
When you see your self entering into a chamber it is figurative of ernest prayer meaning you are called to pray.

ISAIAH 26:20
Go, my people, enter your rooms and shut the doors behind you; hide yourselves for a little while until his wrath has passed by.

CHARIOT
Is a symbol of power

PSALMS 20:7
Some trust in chariots and some in horses, but we trust in the name of the LORD our God.

PSALMS 104:3
and lays the beams of his upper chambers on their waters. He makes the clouds his chariot and rides on the wings of the wind

CITIZENSHIP
Acceptance into God's kingdom.

PHILIPPIANS 3:20
But our citizenship is in heaven. And we eagerly await a Savoir from there, the Lord Jesus Christ,

CLAPPING OF HANDS
Signifies joy.

2 KINGS 11:12
Jehoiada brought out the king's son and put the crown on him; he presented him with a copy of the covenant and proclaimed him king. They anointed him, and the people clapped their hands and shouted, "Long live the king!"

PSALMS 47:1
Clap your hands, all you nations; shout to God with cries of joy.

COLD IN HARVEST
Is a symbol of refreshing like a faithful messenger.

PROVERBS 25:13
Like a snow-cooled drink at harvest time is a trustworthy messenger to the one who sends him; he refreshes the spirit of his master.

CONSULTING SOMEONE WHO IS NOT A MAN OF GOD
Familiar spirit

LEVITICUS 20:27
"A man or woman who is a medium or spiritist among you must be put to death. You are to stone them; their blood will be on their own heads."

COVERING BY THE WATERS OF THE SEA
Is a symbol of diffusion (not concentrated) of spiritual truth over the earth.

ISAIAH 11:9
They will neither harm nor destroy on all my holy mountain, for the earth will be filled with the knowledge of the LORD as the waters cover the sea.

HABAKKUK 2:14
For the earth will be filled with the knowledge of the glory of the LORD as the waters cover the sea.

COVERING UNDER HEAT
Is a sign of protection from the shadow of the Almighty God.

PSALMS 17:8
Keep me as the apple of your eye; hide me in the shadow of your wings.

ISAIAH 49:2
He made my mouth like a sharpened sword, in the shadow of his hand he hid me; he made me into a polished arrow and concealed me in his quiver.

CROWN
Symbol of victory and reward
Emblem of an exalted state

PROVERBS 12:4
A wife of noble character is her husband's crown, but a disgraceful wife is like decay in his bones.

PROVERBS 17:6
Children's children are a crown to the aged, and parents are the pride of their children.

ISAIAH 28:5
In that day the LORD Almighty will be a glorious crown, a beautiful wreath for the remnant of his people.

PHILIPPIANS 4:1
Therefore, my brothers and sisters, you whom I love and long for, my joy and crown, stand firm in the Lord in this way, dear friends!

CUP

Is the general expression for the condition of life either prosperous or miserable.

PSALMS 11:6
On the wicked he will rain fiery coals and burning sulphur; a scorching wind will be their lot.

PSALMS 16:5
LORD, you have assigned me my portion and my cup; you have made my lot secure.

PSALMS 23:5
You prepare a table before me in the presence of my enemies. You anoint my head with oil; my cup overflows.

JEREMIAH 51:7
Babylon was a gold cup in the Lord's hand; she made the whole earth drunk. The nations drank her wine; therefore they have now gone mad.

REVELATION 7:4
Then I heard the number of those who were sealed: 144,000 from all the tribes of Israel.

CUP BEARER

Is a great personality before a king.

NEHEMIAH 1:11
Lord, let your ear be attentive to the prayer of this your servant and to the prayer of your servants who delight in revering your name. Give your servant success today by granting him favour in the presence of this man." I was cupbearer to the king.

NEHEMIAH 2:1
In the month of Nisan in the twentieth year of King Artaxerxes, when wine was brought for him, I took the wine and gave it to the king. I had not been sad in his presence before.

CUP OF BLESSING

When seen in the congregation or church with a prayer invoked upon to drink

1 CORINTHIANS 10:16
Is not the cup of thanksgiving for which we give thanks a participation in the blood of Christ? And is not the bread that we break a participation in the body of Christ?

Therefore a cup has many meanings as seen.

CUP OF CONSOLATION

To console relatives in mourning.

JEREMIAH 16:7
No one will offer food to comfort those who mourn for the dead-not even for a father or a mother-nor will anyone give them a drink to console them.

CUP OF SALVATION
When people are drinking or seeing a cup when people are giving thanks to God.

PSALMS 116:13
I will lift up the cup of salvation and call on the name of the LORD.

NUMBERS 15:5
With each lamb for the burnt offering or the sacrifice, prepare a quarter of a him of wine as a drink offering.

NUMBERS 28:7
The accompanying drink offering is to be a quarter of a hin of fermented drink with each lamb. Pour out the drink offering to the LORD at the sanctuary.

COLOURS

BLACK

i) **As opposite of white denotes the following, mourning, affliction, calamity and death.**

JEREMIAH 14:2
Judah mourns, her cities languish; they wail for the land, and a cry goes up from Jerusalem.

LAMENTATIONS 4:8
But now they are blacker than soot; they are not recognized in the streets. Their skin has shrivelled on their bones; it has become as dry as a stick.

ii) Is a sign of humiliation

MALACHI 3:14
You have said, 'It is futile to serve God. What did we gain by carrying out his requirements and going about like mourners before the LORD Almighty?

iii) Is also an evil omen

ZECHARIAH 6:2
The first chariot had red horses, the second black,

REVELATION 6:5
When the Lamb opened the third seal, I heard the third living creature say, "Come!" I looked, and there before me was a black horse! Its rider was holding a pair of scales in his hand.

BLACK AND WHITE MIXED TOGETHER
Is a sign of lies and truth

BLUE
Divinity or divine

BLUE & PURPLE MIXED

i. **Is a symbol of revelation or divinity.**

ii. **It is the symbol of revealed God**

iii. **It also represents reward and denote the softened divine Majesty condescending to man in grace**

EXODUS 24:10
and saw the God of Israel. Under his feet was something like a pavement made of lapis lazuli, as bright blue as the sky.

EZEKIEL 1:26
Above the vault over their heads was what looked like a throne of lapis lazuli, and high above on the throne was a figure like that of a man.

COLOURS

GREEN
Freshness or new

Is an emblem of freshness, vigour and prosperity

PSALMS 52:8
But I am like an olive tree flourishing in the house of God; I trust in God's unfailing love for ever and ever.

PSALMS 92:14
They will still bear fruit in old age; they will stay fresh and green,

LINEN
Is an emblem of moral purity and of luxury

REVELATION 15:6
Out of the temple came the seven angels with the seven plagues. They were dressed in clean, shining linen and wore golden sashes around their chests.

LUKE 16:19
There was a rich man who was dressed in purple and fine linen and lived in luxury every day.

FINE LINEN OR DULL WHITE
Humanity

PURPLE
Is the dress for kings, it is therefore associated with royalty and majesty

JUDGES 8:26
The weight of the gold rings he asked for came to seventeen hundred shekels, not counting the ornaments, the pendants and the purple garments worn by the kings of Midian or the chains that were on their camels' necks.

ESTHER 8:15
When Mordecai left the king's presence, he was wearing royal garments of blue and white, a large crown of gold and a purple robe of fine linen. And the city of Susa held a joyous celebration.

RED
Is the colour of fire and life. Blood is red because life is a fiery process

RED AND WHITE
Symbolises selfishness, covetousness and passionate life. Red can be sinful

ISAIAH 1:18
Come now, let us reason together," says the LORD. "Though your sins are like scarlet, they shall be as white as

snow; though they are red as crimson, they shall be like wool.

RED AND WHITE MIXED TOGETHER
Is a sign of purity and covenant

RED (CRIMSON)
Represents blood and the life principle of man and beast.

GENESIS 9:4-6
4 *"But you must not eat meat that has its lifeblood still in it.*
5 *And for your lifeblood I will surely demand an accounting. I will demand an accounting from every animal. And from each man, too, I will demand an accounting for the life of his fellow man.*
6 *"Whoever sheds the blood of man, by man shall his blood be shed; for in the image of God has God made man.*

RED
Also represents atonement

ISAIAH 63:2
Why are your garments red, like those of one treading the winepress?

HEBREW 9:22
In fact, the law requires that nearly everything be cleansed

with blood, and without the shedding of blood there is no forgiveness.

WHITE
i. Is a symbol of light, purity or holiness

PSALMS 27:1
The LORD is my light and my salvation- whom shall I fear? The LORD is the stronghold of my life- of whom shall I be afraid?

REVELATION 19:8
Fine linen, bright and clean, was given her to wear." (Fine linen stands for the righteous acts of God's people.)

MATTHEW 17:2
There he was transfigured before them. His face shone like the sun, and his clothes became as white as the light.

ii. Is a sign of festivity

ECCLESIASTES 9:8
Always be clothed in white, and always anoint your head with oil.

iii. Is a sign of triumph

ZECHARIAH 6:3
the third white, and the fourth dappled-all of them powerful.

COLOURS

REVELATION 6:2

I looked, and there before me was a white horse! Its rider held a bow, and he was given a crown, and he rode out as a conqueror bent on conquest.

iv) Is a symbol of glory and majesty

DANIEL 7:9

As I looked, "thrones were set in place, and the Ancient of Days took his seat. His clothing was as white as snow; the hair of his head was white like wool. His throne was flaming with fire, and its wheels were all ablaze.

EZEKIEL 9:3

Now the glory of the God of Israel went up from above the cherubim, where it had been, and moved to the threshold of the temple. Then the LORD called to the man clothed in linen who had the writing kit at his side

MATTHEW 28:3

His appearance was like lightning, and his clothes were white as snow.

John 20:12

and saw two angels in white, seated where Jesus' body had been, one at the head and the other at the foot.

DIVIDING WALL
Means separation of two people or groups of people.

EPHESIANS 2:14
For he himself is our peace, who has made the two one and has destroyed the barrier, the dividing wall of hostility,

DAY
Means a whole term of life considered as a season of active labour
Means a definite period or something destined to happen.

JOHN 9:4
As long as it is day, we must do the works of him who sent me. Night is coming, when no one can work

GENESIS 2:4
This is the account of the heavens and the earth when they were created, when the LORD God made the earth and the heavens.

DEAD BODIES DUMP AND BURNT
Signifies lost spirits and souls for their eternal state
2 KINGS 23:13-14
13 *The king also desecrated the high places that were east of Jerusalem on the south of the Hill of Corruption-the ones Solomon king of Israel had built for Ashtoreth the vile goddess of the Sidonians, for Chemosh the vile god of Moab, and for Molek the detestable god of the people of Ammon.*
14 *Josiah smashed the sacred stones and cut down the Asherah poles and covered the sites with human bones.*

DEEP WATER
Means counsel in the heart and word of wisdom.

PROVERBS 20:5
The purposes of a man's heart are deep waters, but a man of understanding draws them out.

PROVERBS 18:4
The words of a man's mouth are deep waters, but the fountain of wisdom is a bubbling brook.

DIFFICULTIES TO STOP WATER
Is a symbol of strive and contention.

PROVERBS 17:14
Starting a quarrel is like breaching a dam; so drop the matter before a dispute breaks out.

DOG
Lustfulness and vagabond.

PSALMS 59:6 &14
6 They return at evening, snarling like dogs, and prowl about the city.
14 They return at evening, snarling like dogs, and prowl about the city.

DONKEYS
A time to plough or go back to work.

ISAIAH 30:24
The oxen and donkeys that work the soil will eat fodder and mash, spread out with fork and shovel

DONKEY ROAMING
Is a sign of liberation.

DOVE
Reconciliation of God and peace

GENESIS 8:8-10
8 Then he sent out a dove to see if the water had receded from the surface of the ground.
9 But the dove could find nowhere to perch because there was water over all the surface of the earth; so it returned to Noah in the ark. He reached out his hand and took the dove and brought it back to himself in the ark.
10 He waited seven more days and again sent out the dove from the ark.

DRAGON
Meaning - Satan, symbol of sin.

REVELATION 12:3-4
3 Then another sign appeared in heaven: an enormous red dragon with seven heads and ten horns and seven crowns on its heads.
4 Its tail swept a third of the stars out of the sky and flung them to the earth. The dragon stood in front of the woman who was about to give birth, so that it might devour her child the moment he was born.

REVELATION 16:13
Then I saw three evil spirits that looked like frogs; they came out of the mouth of the dragon, out of the mouth of the beast and out of the mouth of the false prophet.

REVELATION 20:2
He seized the dragon, that ancient serpent, who is the devil, or Satan, and bound him for a thousand years.

DRINKING FROM A WELL
Is a sign of domestic happiness.

PROVERBS 15:15
All the days of the oppressed are wretched, but the cheerful heart has a continual feast.

DRY LEAF
Symbolises scarcity and lack, adversity and decay.

JOB 13:25
Will you torment a windblown leaf? Will you chase after dry chaff?

Isaiah 64:6
All of us have become like one who is unclean, and all our righteous acts are like filthy rags; we all shrivel up like a leaf, and like the wind our sins sweep us away.

DIGGING A PIT
Making a plot of mischief. Also means great discomfort, starvation and punishment.

PROVERBS 26:27
If anyone digs a pit, they themselves will fall into it; if anyone rolls a stone, it will roll back on them.

REVELATION 9:1-2
1 *The fifth angel sounded his trumpet, and I saw a star that had fallen from the sky to the earth. The star was given the key to the shaft of the Abyss.*
2 *When he opened the Abyss, smoke rose from it like the smoke from a gigantic furnace. The sun and sky were darkened by the smoke from the Abyss.*

EAGLE
Is a symbol of power or a powerful king

EZEKIEL 17:3
Say to them, 'This is what the Sovereign LORD says: A great eagle with powerful wings, long feathers and full plumage of varied colours came to Lebanon. Taking hold of the top of a cedar.

PSALMS 103:5
who satisfies your desires with good things so that your youth is renewed like the eagle's

ISAIAH 40:31
but those who hope in the LORD will renew their strength. They will soar on wings like eagles; they will run and not grow weary, they will walk and not be faint.

EAGLE'S FLYING SWIFTLY IN THE AIR
i) **Is a sign of riches melting away**

PROVERBS 23:5
Cast but a glance at riches, and they are gone, for they will surely sprout wings and fly off to the sky like an eagle.

ii) **It also means rapid movement of armies**

DEUTERONOMY 24:7
If someone is caught kidnapping another Israelite and treating or selling that Israelite as a slave, the kidnapper must die. You must purge the evil from among you.

JEREMIAH 4:13
Look! He advances like the clouds, his chariots come like a whirlwind, his horses are swifter than eagles. Woe to us! We are ruined!

iii) **It also symbolises the swiftness of mans days**

JOB 9:26
They skim past like boats of papyrus, like eagles swooping down on their prey.

EARTH QUAKE
Symbol of God's Judgement

ISAIAH 24:20
The earth reels like a drunkard, it sways like a hut in the wind; so heavy upon it is the guilt of its rebellion that it falls-never to rise again.

REVELATION 8:5
Then the angel took the censer, filled it with fire from the altar,

and hurled it on the earth; and there came peals of thunder, rumblings, flashes of lightning and an earthquake.

EATING ASHES
Is an expression of deepest misery and degradation.

Psalms 102:4
My heart is blighted and withered like grass; I forget to eat my food.

Isaiah 44:20
Such people feed on ashes, a deluded heart misleads them; they cannot save themselves, or say, "Is not this thing in my right hand a lie?"

F

FAMINE
Withdrawal of God's word and destruction of idols.

ZEPHANIAH 2:11
The Lord will be terrifying to them, for He will starve all the gods of the earth; and all the coastlands of the nations will bow down to Him, everyone from his own place.

AMOS 8:11- 12
11 *"The days are coming," declares the Sovereign LORD, "when I will send a famine through the land- not a famine of food or a thirst for water, but a famine of hearing the words of the LORD.*
12 *People will stagger from sea to sea and wander from north to east, searching for the word of the LORD, but they will not find it.*

FANNING
Is a sign of God scattering our enemies

ISAIAH 41:16
You will winnow them, the wind will pick them up, and a gale will blow them away. But you will rejoice in the LORD and glory in the Holy One of Israel.

FAT
Meaning - Good health and vigour.

I believe you have heard before, the fat of the land , fat of the lamb and fat of products etc. It is close to the blood flow.

LEVITICUS 17:14
Because the life of every creature is its blood. That is why I have said to the Israelites, "You must not eat the blood of any creature, because the life of every creature is its blood; anyone who eats it must be cut off."

FENCE
Means enclosure or protection
Fences were built of stones to protect cultivated lands, sheepfolds etc. Serpents hid in the crevices of such fences.

PSALMS 62:3
How long will you assault me? Would all of you throw me down- this leaning wall, this tottering fence?

ECCLESIASTES 10:8
Whoever digs a pit may fall into it; whoever breaks through a wall may be bitten by a snake.

AMOS 5:19
It will be as though a man fled from a lion only to meet a bear, as though he entered his house and rested his hand on the wall only to have a snake bite him.

FINGER
Special and agency of anyone.

EXODUS 8:19
The magicians said to Pharaoh, "This is the finger of God." But Pharaoh's heart was hard and he would not listen, just as the LORD had said.

EXODUS 31:18
When the LORD finished speaking to Moses on Mount Sinai, he gave him the two tablets of the covenant law, the tablets of stone inscribed by the finger of God.

PSALMS 8:3
When I consider your heavens, the work of your fingers, the moon and the stars, which you have set in place.

LUKE 11:20
But if I drive out demons by the finger of God, then the kingdom of God has come upon you.

FIRE
Is a symbol of God's presence and the instrument of his power in the way of approval or destruction depending on what you see.

EXODUS 14:19
Then the angel of God, who had been travelling in front of Israel's army, withdrew and went behind them. The pillar of cloud also moved from in front and stood behind them,

EXODUS 3:2
There the angel of the LORD appeared to him in flames of fire from within a bush. Moses saw that though the bush was on fire it did not burn up.

ISAIAH 6:4-5
4 *At the sound of their voices the doorposts and thresholds shook and the temple was filled with smoke.*
5 *"Woe to me!" I cried. "I am ruined! For I am a man of unclean lips, and I live among a people of unclean lips, and my eyes have seen the King, the LORD Almighty."*

EZEKIEL 1:4-5
4 *I looked, and I saw a windstorm coming out of the north - an immense cloud with flashing*

lightning and surrounded by brilliant light. The center of the fire looked like glowing metal,
5 and in the fire was what looked like four living creatures. In appearance their form was human,

REVELATION 1:12-14
12 *I turned around to see the voice that was speaking to me. And when I turned I saw seven golden lamp stands,*
13 *and among the lamp stands was someone like a son of man, dressed in a robe reaching down to his feet and with a golden sash around his chest.*
14 *The hair on his head was white like wool, as white as snow, and his eyes were like blazing fire.*

FIRST BORN
Is an expression of excellence

HEBREWS 12:23
to the church of the firstborn, whose names are written in heaven. You have come to God, the Judge of all, to the spirits of the righteous made perfect,

ISAIAH 14:30
The poorest of the poor will find pasture, and the needy will lie down in safety. But your root I

will destroy by famine; it will slay your survivors.

JOB18:13
It eats away parts of his skin; death's firstborn devours his limbs.

FISH
Invisible church or disciples of Christ.

MATTHEW 4:18-19
18 *As Jesus was walking beside the Sea of Galilee, he saw two brothers, Simon called Peter and his brother Andrew. They were casting a net into the lake, for they were fishermen.*
19 *"Come, follow me," Jesus said, "and I will send you out to fish for people."*

FISH CAUGHT IN A NET
Men overtaken suddenly by evil.

ECCLESIASTES 9:12
Moreover, no one knows when their hour will come: As fish are caught in a cruel net or birds are taken in a snare, so people are trapped by evil times that fall unexpectedly upon them.

LAMENTATIONS 1:13
From on high he sent fire, sent it down into my bones. He spread a net for my feet and turned me

back. He made me desolate,
faint all the day long.

EZEKIEL 12:13

*I will spread my net for him, and
he will be caught in my snare; I
will bring him to Babylonia, the
land of the Chaldeans, but he will
not see it, and there he will die.*

HOSEA 7:12

*When they go, I will throw my
net over them; I will pull them
down like the birds in the sky.
When I hear them flocking
together, I will catch them.*

FISH GATE

**A door opened for believers of
Christ.**

NEHEMIAH 3:3

*The Fish Gate was rebuilt by the
sons of Hassenaah. They laid its
beams and put its doors and
bolts and bars in place.*

FISHING

**Evangelism to bring people to
follow Christ**

MATTHEW 4:18

*As Jesus was walking beside the
Sea of Galilee, he saw two
brothers, Simon called Peter and
his brother Andrew. They were
casting a net into the lake, for
they were fishermen.*

FLAMMING TORCH

**Is a figure and symbol of great
anger and destruction.**

ZECHARIAH 12:6

*"On that day I will make the
clans of Judah like a fire pot in a
woodpile, like a flaming torch
among sheaves. They will
consume right and left all the
surrounding peoples, but
Jerusalem will remain intact in
her place.*

ROMANS 13:11-12

11 *And do this, understanding
the present time. The hour has
already come for you to wake up
from your slumber, because our
salvation is nearer now than
when we first believed.*
12 *The night is nearly over; the
day is almost here. So let us put
aside the deeds of darkness and
put on the armour of light.*

EPHESIANS 5:14

*This is why it is said: Wake up,
sleeper, rise from the dead, and
Christ will shine on you."*

1 CORINTHIANS 11:30

*That is why many among you are
weak and sick, and a number of
you have fallen asleep*

F

FLINT STONE
Is an indication of a sword for a divine purpose

EXODUS 4:25
But Zipporah took a flint knife, cut off her son's foreskin and touched Moses' feet with it. "Surely you are a bridegroom of blood to me," she said.

JOSHUA 5:2-3
2 At that time the LORD said to Joshua, "Make flint knives and circumcise the Israelites again."
3 So Joshua made flint knives and circumcised the Israelites at Gibeath Haaraloth

FLOOD
Catastrophic event of evil.

ISAIAH 59:19
From the west, people will fear the name of the LORD, and from the rising of the sun, they will revere his glory. For he will come like a pent-up flood that the breath of the LORD drives along.

FLOWERS' READINESS OF DECAY
Means - Shortness of human life

JOB 14:2
They spring up like flowers and wither away; like fleeting shadows, they do not endure.

PSALMS 103:15
As for mortals, their days are like grass, they flourish like a flower of the field;

1 PETER 1:24
For, "All people are like grass, and all their glory is like the flowers of the field; the grass withers and the flowers fall,

FOREST
Is a city or a kingdom.

EZEKIEL 20:46
"Son of man, set your face toward the south; preach against the south and prophesy against the forest of the southland.

FOREST BURNING
Is a kingdom or a nation under God's judgement.

FORNICATION OR ADULTERY
Is a sign of insecurity, deprivation and defiling of the mind to prevent relationship with God.

2 CORINTHIANS 11:2
I am jealous for you with a godly jealousy. I promised you to one husband, to Christ, so that I might present you as a pure virgin to him.

REVELATION 2:21
I have given her time to repent of her immorality, but she is unwilling.

REVELATION 14:8
A second angel followed and said, "'Fallen! Fallen is Babylon the Great,' which made all the nations drink the maddening wine of her adulteries."

MATTHEW 5:28
But I tell you that anyone who looks at a woman lustfully has already committed adultery with her in his heart.

FORTRESS
A divine protection to those who trust in the Lord.

2 SAMUEL 22:2
He said:" The LORD is my rock, my fortress and my deliverer;

FOUNTAIN
i) Is a natural source of water. It means prosperity

DEUTERONOMY 33:28
So Israel will live in safety; Jacob will dwell [a] secure in a land of grain and new wine, where the heavens drop dew.

ii) It also means a good wife

PROVERBS 5:18
May your fountain be blessed, and may you rejoice in the wife of your youth.

iii) Means spiritual wisdom

PROVERBS 16:22
Prudence is a fountain of life to the prudent, but folly brings punishment to fools.

iv) God and Christ as the source in which you stand.

MATTHEW 13:35
So was fulfilled what was spoken through the prophet: "I will open my mouth in parables, I will utter things hidden since the creation of the world."

FRUIT
Off springs or children

PSALMS 127 :3
Children are heritage from the Lord, offspring a reward from him.

G

GAP
A sign of separation or corruption

EZEKIEL 22:30
"I looked for someone among them who would build up the wall and stand before me in the gap on behalf of the land so I would not have to destroy it, but I found no one.

GATE
Means a city.

GENESIS 22:17
I will surely bless you and make your descendants as numerous as the stars in the sky and as the sand on the seashore. Your descendants will take possession of the cities of their enemies,

GATES - (GATES OF RIGHTEOUSNESS) WHEN ENTERING INTO A CHURCH
Meaning - a door way to your future

PSALMS 118:19
Open for me the gates of the righteous; I will enter and give thanks to the LORD

GATES OF DEATH
Is a symbol of death. Gates leading to death or war zone or into darkness.

JOB 38:17
Have the gates of death been shown to you? Have you seen the gates of the deepest darkness?

PSALMS 9:13
LORD, see how my enemies persecute me! Have mercy and lift me up from the gates of death.

GATES OF HADES
Gates of Hades or underworld. A symbol of empire and power

MATTHEW 16:18
And I tell you that you are Peter, [b] and on this rock I will build my church, and the gates of death will not overcome it.

GIRDLE
Means readiness for service that may be required.
Is also a symbol of strength, activity and power

1 PETER 1:13
Therefore, with minds that are alert and fully sober, set your hope on the grace to be brought to you when Jesus Christ is revealed at his coming.

JOB 12:18
He takes off the shackles put on by kings and ties a loincloth around their waist.

GIRDLING WITH MOURNING CLOTHES
Is a figure of affliction.

PSALMS 35:13
Yet when they were ill, I put on sackcloth and humbled myself with fasting. When my prayers returned to me unanswered,

GNATS
Blood sucking virus or diseases. Means do not ignore small tiny sins to deal with weightier matters

MATTHEW 23:24
You blind guides! You strain out a gnat but swallow a camel.

GOAT
Meaning - Wicked Conception (Demons)

LEVITICUS 17:7
They must no longer offer any of their sacrifices to the goat idols to whom they prostitute themselves. This is to be a lasting ordinance for them and for the generations to come.'

REVELATIONS 18:2
With a mighty voice he shouted: 'Fallen! Fallen is Babylon the Great!' She has become a dwelling for demons and a haunt for every evil spirit, a haunt for every unclean bird, a haunt for every unclean and detestable animal.

GOING DOWN INTO A PIT
Dying without hope or going to the place of the dead.

PSALMS 28:1
To you, LORD, I call; you are my Rock, do not turn a deaf ear to me. For if you remain silent, I will be like those who go down to the pit.

PSALMS 30:3-9
3 You, LORD, brought me up from the realm of the dead; you spared me from going down to the pit.
4 Sing the praises of the LORD, you his faithful people; praise his holy name.
5 For his anger lasts only a moment, but his favour lasts a lifetime; weeping may remain for a night, but rejoicing comes in the morning.
6 When I felt secure, I said, "I will never be shaken."

7 LORD, when you favoured me, you made my royal mountain stand firm; but when you hid your face, I was dismayed.
8 To you, LORD, I called; to the Lord I cried for mercy:
9 "What is gained if I am silenced, if I go down to the pit? Will the dust praise you? Will it proclaim your faithfulness?

GRAVES AND DEPTHS
Signifies death and misery

GRAVEYARD
Symbolises isolation, loneliness, hurt, pain and death

MARK 5:2-3
2 When Jesus got out of the boat, a man with an evil spirit came from the tombs to meet him.
3 This man lived in the tombs, and no one could bind him anymore, not even with a chain.

GREEN LEAF
Is outward manifestation of life, a fresh bright coloured leaf shows rich nourishment of a person.

It symbolises prosperity of a person.

PSALMS 1:3
They are like a tree planted by streams of water, which yields its fruit in season and whose leaf does not wither- whatever they do prospers.

JEREMIAH 17:8
They will be like a tree planted by the water that sends out its roots by the stream. It does not fear when heat comes; its leaves are always green. It has no worries in a year of drought and never fails to bear fruit."

GIVING A HAND
Is a sign of submission

2 CHRONICLES 30:8
Do not be stiff-necked, as your parents were; submit to the LORD. Come to his sanctuary, which he has consecrated forever. Serve the LORD your God, so that his fierce anger will turn away from you.

HAILING

Symbolises divine vengeance upon kingdoms and nations or your enemies

ISAIAH 32:19
Though hail flattens the forest and the city is levelled completely.

ISAIAH 28:2-17
2 See, the Lord has one who is powerful and strong. Like a hailstorm and a destructive wind, like a driving rain and a flooding downpour, he will throw it forcefully to the ground. I will make justice the measuring line and righteousness the plumb line; hail will sweep away your refuge, the lie, and water will overflow your hiding place.

HAGGAI 2:17
I struck all the work of your hands with blight, mildew and hail, yet you did not return to me,' declares the LORD.

HAIR GRAY

Is a symbol of honour, respect and authority.

PROVERBS 16:31
Gray hair is a crown of splendour; it is attained by a righteous life.

HAND

Hands have different figurative meanings and so let me take it at a time and see when it means the hand of God or man.
A hand symbolises ACTIVE SERVICE

HAND (RIGHT)
Symbol of power and strength.

EXODUS 15:6
Your right hand, LORD, was majestic in power. Your right hand, LORD, shattered the enemy.

HAND ON THE PLOW
Is a sign consistency.

LUKE 9:62
Jesus replied, "No one who puts a hand to the plow and looks back is fit for service in the kingdom of God."

HANDS COVERED WITH BLOOD
Cruelty

HANDS LIFTED UP
Prayers being offered.

JOB 11:13
Yet if you devote your heart to him and stretch out your hands to him.

1 TIMOTHY 2:8
Therefore I want the men everywhere to pray, lifting up holy hands without anger or disputing.

HANDS, SOUL, EYES OR HEART LIFTED TO THE LORD
Is an expression of sentiments and emotions of one who prays earnestly or ardently desires something.

HANDS PUT TOGETHER ON THE HEAD
Signifies extreme grief

2 SAMUEL 13:19
Tamar put ashes on her head and tore the ornamented robe she was wearing. She put her hands on her head and went away, weeping aloud as she went.

JEREMIAH 2:37
You will also leave that place with your hands on your head, for the LORD has rejected those you trust; you will not be helped by them.

HANDS OPEN
Is a sign of liberality

DEUTERONOMY 15:8
Rather, be open handed and freely lend them whatever they need.

PSALMS 104:28
When you give it to them, they gather it up; when you open your hand, they are satisfied with good things.

HANDS CLOSED
Is a sign of lack

DEUTERONOMY 15:7
If anyone is poor among your people in any of the towns of the land that the LORD your God is giving you, do not be hardhearted or tight-fisted toward them.

HAND WITHDRAWN
Means - Withdrawing support

PSALMS 74:11
Why do you hold back your hand, your right hand? Take it from the folds of your garment and destroy them!

HAND WASHED
Symbol of innocence.

HAND CUT
Is expression of self denial.

MATTHEW 5:30
And if your right hand causes you to stumble, cut it off and throw it away. It is better for you to lose one part of your body than for your whole body to go into hell.

HARVEST
i. Is a sign of judgement

JEREMIAH 51:33
This is what the LORD Almighty, the God of Israel, says: "Daughter Babylon is like a threshing floor at the time it is trampled; the time to harvest her will soon come."

HOSEA 6:11
"Also for you, Judah, a harvest is appointed."Whenever I would restore the fortunes of my people,

ii. A time to receive the gospel.

JOEL 3:13
Swing the sickle, for the harvest is ripe. Come, trample the grapes, for the winepress is full and the vats overflow- so great is their wickedness!"

iii. A season of grace

JEREMIAH 8:20
The harvest is past, the summer has ended, and we are not saved.

iv. The season of the age.

MATTHEW 13:39
and the enemy who sows them is the devil. The harvest is the end of the age, and the harvesters are angels.

ISAIAH 18:4
This is what the LORD says to me: "I will remain quiet and will look on from my dwelling place, like shimmering heat in the sunshine, like a cloud of dew in the heat of harvest."

HEAD
As the head is an illustration of God, however it symbolises other things depending on what you see or its application.

It may symbolise

i. A Ruler

DANIEL 2:38
In your hands he has placed all people everywhere and the beasts of the field and the birds in the sky. Wherever they live, he has made you ruler over them all. You are that head of gold.

ii. Chief Men

ISAIAH 9:14-15
14 *So the LORD will cut off from Israel both head and tail, both palm branch and reed in a single day;*
15 *the elders and dignitaries are the head, the prophets who teach lies are the tail.*

iii. A chief city of a kingdom.

ISAIAH 7:8
For the head of Aram is Damascus, and the head of Damascus is only Rezin. Within sixty-five years Ephraim will be too shattered to be a people.

HEAD ANOINTED
Is a symbol of joy and prosperity

PSALM 23:5
You prepare a table before me in the presence of my enemies. You anoint my head with oil; my cup overflows.

HEAD BOWING
Sign of worship

GENESIS 43:28
They replied, "Your servant our father is still alive and well." And they bowed down, prostrating themselves before him.

HEAD CUT OFF
Is a sign of defeat

JUDGES 5:21
The river Kishon swept them away, the age-old river, the river Kishon. March on, my soul; be strong!

1 SAMUEL 17:51 & 57
51 *David ran and stood over him. He took hold of the Philistine's sword and drew it from the sheath. After he killed him, he cut off his head with the sword. When the Philistines saw that their hero was dead, they turned and ran.*
57 *As soon as David returned from killing the Philistine, Abner took him and brought him before Saul, with David still holding the Philistine's head*

HEAD LIFTED UP
Signifies joy, confidence and exaltation

PSALMS 3:3
But you, LORD, are a shield around me, my glory, the one who lifts my head high.

LUKE 21:28
When these things begin to take place, stand up and lift up your heads, because your redemption is drawing near."

GENESIS 40:13
Within three days Pharaoh will lift up your head and restore you to your position and you will put Pharaoh's cup in his hand, just as you used to do when you were his cupbearer.

HEAD MADE BALD
Signifies heavy judgement.

ISAIAH 3:24
Instead of fragrance there will be a stench; instead of a sash, a rope; instead of well-dressed hair, baldness; instead of fine clothing, sackcloth; instead of beauty, branding.

ISAIAH 15:2
Dibon goes up to its temple to its high places to weep; Moab wails over Nebo and Medeba. Every head is shaved and every beard cut off.

MICAH 1:16
Shave your head in mourning for the children in whom you delight; make yourself as bald as the vulture, for they will go from you into exile

HEAD SHAKING OR WAGGING
Is a gesture of mockery at another's fall or misfortune.

ISAIAH 37:22
This is the word the LORD has spoken against him: "Virgin Daughter Zion despises and mocks you. Daughter Jerusalem tosses her head as you flee.

HEAD COVERED
Is a symbol of defence and protection or of subjection

PSALMS 104:7
But at your rebuke the waters fled, at the sound of your thunder they took to flight;

1 CORINTHIANS 11:5 &10
5 *But every woman who prays or prophesies with her head uncovered dishonours her head- it is the same as having her head shaved.*
10 *It is for this reason that a woman ought to have authority over her own head, because of the angels*

HEAD SHAVING
Meaning- Hard Judgement and departure of glory.

ISAIAH 3:24
Instead of fragrance there will be a stench; instead of a sash, a rope; instead of well-dressed hair, baldness; instead of fine clothing, sackcloth; instead of beauty, branding.

HEAD SEALED

Is to prevent one from working

JOB 37:7

So that all men he has made may know his work , he stops every man from his labour.

HEAP OF STONES

Is a sign of making a peace treaty.

GENESIS 31:46

He said to his relatives, "Gather some stones." So they took stones and piled them in a heap, and they ate there by the heap.

HEAP OF STONES ON A GRAVE

Is a sign of a treaty over a notorious offender.

JOSHUA 7:26

Over Achan they heaped up a large pile of rocks, which remains to this day. Then the LORD turned from his fierce anger. Therefore that place has been called the Valley of Achor ever since.

HEIFER

Is a young cow when treading on grains without a headstall.

An expression of stubbornness without control / to resist authority.

HOSEA 4:16

The Israelites are stubborn, like a stubborn heifer. How then can the LORD pasture them like lambs in a meadow?

HEIFER THAT LOVES TO THRESH

Is an expression of choosing pleasant productive and profitable labour which allows to eat with pleasure

DEUTERONOMY 25:4

Do not muzzle an ox while it is treading out the grain.

HOLDING A NOSE

Restraining, control and humiliation

2 KINGS 19:28

Because you rage against me and because your insolence has reached my ears, I will put my hook in your nose and my bit in your mouth, and I will make you return by the way you came.'

HOLDING BY RIGHT HAND

Expressing support

PSALMS 73:23

Yet I am always with you; you hold me by my right hand.

HONEY AND MILK
Means the Word of God

PSALMS 19:10
They are more precious than gold, than much pure gold; they are sweeter than honey, than honey from the honeycomb.

PSALMS 119:103
How sweet are your words to my taste, sweeter than honey to my mouth!

HORN BRINGING DOWN
Is a sign of degrading

JOB 16:15
"I have sewed sackcloth over my skin and buried my brow in the dust."

HORNS BUDDING OR SPROUTING
Means commencement of power or revival of a nation

PSALMS 132:17
"Here I will make a horn grow for David and set up a lamp for my anointed one."

EZEKIEL 29:21
"On that day I will make a horn grow for the house of Israel, and I will open your mouth among them. Then they will know that I am the LORD."

HORN EXALTING
Increase of power or glory

1 SAMUEL 2:10
those who oppose the LORD will be broken. The Most High will thunder from heaven; the LORD will judge the ends of the earth. "He will give strength to his king and exalt the horn of his anointed."

PSALMS 89:17
For you are their glory and strength, and by your favour you exalt our horn.

HORN PUSHING
It signifies conquest

DEUTERONOMY 33:17
In majesty he is like a firstborn bull; his horns are the horns of a wild ox. With them he will gore the nations, even those at the ends of the earth. Such are the ten thousands of Ephraim; such are the thousands of Manasseh.

2 KINGS 22:1
Josiah was eight years old when he became king, and he reigned in Jerusalem thirty-one years. His mother's name was Jedidah daughter of Adaiah; she was from Bozkath.

H

HORN RAISING OR RISING UP

Arrogance or pride

PSALMS 75:4-5&10

4 To the arrogant I say, 'Boast no more,' and to the wicked, 'Do not lift up your horns.
5 Do not lift your horns against heaven; do not speak with outstretched neck.'"

10 who says, "I will cut off the horns of all the wicked, but the horns of the righteous will be lifted up."

HYSSOP

Is figurative of soul cleansing

PSALMS 51:7

Cleanse me with hyssop, and I will be clean; wash me, and I will be whiter than snow.

INCENSE
Means - Prayer

PSALMS 141:2

May my prayer be set before you like incense; may the lifting up of my hands be like the evening sacrifice.

INCENSE BURNING
Is a type of prayer

PSALMS 141:2

May my prayer be set before you like incense; may the lifting up of my hands be like the evening sacrifice.

REVELATION 5:8

And when he had taken it, the four living creatures and the twenty-four elders fell down before the Lamb. Each one had a harp and they were holding golden bowls full of incense, which are the prayers of God's people.

INSULT
Means - curse

EXODUS 22:28

Do not blaspheme God or curse the ruler of your people

MATTHEW 18:18

Truly I tell you, whatever you bind on earth will be bound in heaven, and whatever you loose on earth will be loosed in heaven.

REVELATION 3:7

To the angel of the church in Philadelphia write: These are the words of him who is holy and true, who holds the key of David. What he opens no one can shut, and what he shuts no one can open.

ISAIAH 22:22

I will place on his shoulder the key to the house of David; what he opens no one can shut, and what he shuts no one can open.

IRON
Is used as a symbol of strength, stubbornness, severe affliction of a hard barren soil or harsh exercise of power

DANIEL 2:33

its legs of iron, its feet partly of iron and partly of baked clay.

DEUTERONOMY 4:20

But as for you, the LORD took you and brought you out of the iron-smelting furnace, out of Egypt, to be the people of his inheritance, as you now are.

REVELATION 2:27

they 'will rule them with an iron

scepter and will dash them to pieces like pottery' - just as I have received authority from my Father.

IRON TOOTH
Is a symbol of destructive power.

DANIEL 7:19
"Then I wanted to know the meaning of the fourth beast, which was different from all the others and most terrifying, with its iron teeth and bronze claws- the beast that crushed and devoured its victims and trampled underfoot whatever was left

J

JOINING OF HANDS
Treaties made or sureties entered or peace agreements.

2 KINGS 11:12

Jehoiada brought out the king's son and put the crown on him; he presented him with a copy of the covenant and proclaimed him king. They anointed him, and the people clapped their hands and shouted, "Long live the king!"

JOB 17:3

Give me, O God, the pledge you demand. Who else will put up security for me?

K

KEY

Is a sign of authority and power

MATTHEW 16:19
I give you the keys of the kingdom of heaven; whatever you bind on earth will be bound in heaven, and whatever you loose on earth will be loosed in heaven.

KIDNAP

Cease of liberty and freedom

EXODUS 21:16
Anyone who kidnaps someone is to be put to death, whether the victim has been sold or is still in the kidnapper's possession.

DEUTERONOMY 24:7
If someone is caught kidnapping another Israelite and treating or selling that Israelite as a slave, the kidnapper must die. You must purge the evil from among you.

1 TIMOTHY 1:10
for the sexually immoral, for those practicing homosexuality, for slave traders and liars and perjurers. And it is for whatever else is contrary to the sound doctrine

KIDNEYS

In dreams when kidneys are mentioned or operated or removed or replaced, it means many things.
They are a seat of desires, provision of knowledge and understanding

JOB 19:27
I myself will see him with my own eyes - I, and not another. How my heart yearns within me!

JOB 16:13
his archers surround me. Without pity, he pierces my kidneys and spills my gall on the ground.

PSALMS 16:7
I will praise the LORD, who counsels me; even at night my heart instructs me

JEREMIAH 12:2
You have planted them, and they have taken root; they grow and bear fruit. You are always on their lips but far from their hearts.

KNEELING

Signifies breaking down to invoke God's blessing.

2 CHRONICLES 6:13

Now he had made a bronze platform, five cubits long, five cubits wide and three cubits high, and had placed it in the centre of the outer court. He stood on the platform and then knelt down before the whole assembly of Israel and spread out his hands toward heaven

DANIEL 6:10

Now when Daniel learned that the decree had been published, he went home to his upstairs room where the windows opened toward Jerusalem. Three times a day he got down on his knees and prayed, giving thanks to his God, just as he had done before.

To kneel also signifies saluting in connection to a blessing.

2 KINGS 4:29

Elisha said to Gehazi, "Tuck your cloak into your belt, take my staff in your hand and run If you meet anyone , do not greet him and if anyone greets you, do not answer. Lay my Staff on the boy's face.

KNEELING BEFORE LARGE STONES

Is idol worship

ISAIAH 57:6

The idols among the smooth stones of the ravines are your portion; they, they are your lot. Yes, to them you have poured out drink offerings and offered grain offerings. In view of all this, should I relent?

LEVITICUS 26:1

'Do not make idols or set up an image or a sacred stone for yourselves, and do not place a carved stone in your land to bow down before it. I am the LORD your God.

KNEES

Symbolic for persons, however have different similitude.

JOB 4:4

Your words have supported those who stumbled; you have strengthened faltering knees.

HEBREWS 12:12

Therefore, strengthen your feeble arms and weak knees

L

LADDER
Is an open door to opportunities and promotion

GENESIS 28:12
He had a dream in which he saw a stairway resting on the earth, with its top reaching to heaven, and the angels of God were ascending and descending on it.

LAMP
Symbolises the WORD OF GOD or Salvation of God.

PSALM 119:105
Your word is a lamp to my feet and a light for my path.

LARGE STONE ON A CAVE
Is a sign of closing an opportunity or opening of the enemies or death depending on what you saw.

MATTHEW 27:60
and placed it in his own new tomb that he had cut out of the rock. He rolled a big stone in front of the entrance to the tomb and went away.

JOSHUA 10:18
he said, "Roll large rocks up to the mouth of the cave, and post some guards there.

LARGE STONES SET UP OR HEAPED
Is a sign of commemorating a remarkable event.

GENESIS 28:18
Early the next morning Jacob took the stone he had placed under his head and set it up as a pillar and poured oil on top of it.

GENESIS 31:45
So Jacob took a stone and set it up as a pillar.

JOSHUA 4:9
Joshua set up the twelve stones that had been in the middle of the Jordan at the spot where the priests who carried the ark of the covenant had stood. And they are there to this day.

LAUGHTER
Means mockery or sometimes JOY. It also means despise, disregard or paying no attention to the person or the subject.

GENESIS 21:6
Sarah said, "God has brought me laughter, and everyone who hears about this will laugh with me."

ECCLESIASTES 3:4
A time to weep and a time to laugh, a time to mourn and a time to dance.

L

GENESIS 18:13
Then the LORD said to Abraham, "Why did Sarah laugh and say, 'Will I really have a child, now that I am old?'

PROVERBS 1:26
I in turn will laugh when disaster strikes you; I will mock when calamity overtakes you-

LAYING HANDS
Means - Blessing

LAZINESS
A person who is not improving his / her opportunities.

PROVERBS 12:27
The lazy do not roast any game, but the diligent feed on the riches of the hunt.

LEANING UPON ANOTHER'S HAND
Is a mark of familiarity and superiority

2 KINGS 5:18
But may the LORD forgive your servant for this one thing: When my master enters the temple of Rimmon to bow down and he is leaning on my arm and I have to bow there also-when I bow down

in the temple of Rimmon, may the LORD forgive your servant for this."

2 KINGS 7:17
Now the king had put the officer on whose arm he leaned in charge of the gate, and the people trampled him in the gateway, and he died, just as the man of God had foretold when the king came down to his house.

LEFT HAND POINTING A DIRECTION
Indicates - Northward

2 SAMUEL 24:5
After crossing the Jordan, they camped near Aroer, south of the town in the gorge, and then went through Gad and on to Jazer.

LEG UNCOVERED
Laying all feminine modesty aside.

ISAIAH 47:2
Take millstones and grind flour; take off your veil. Lift up your skirts, bare your legs, and wade through the streams.

L

LEOPARD
Is an illustration of God in His Judgements.

HOSEA 13:7
So I will come upon them like a lion, like a leopard I will lurk by the path.

DANIEL 7:6
"After that, I looked, and there before me was another beast, one that looked like a leopard. And on its back it had four wings like those of a bird. This beast had four heads, and it was given authority to rule.

REVELATION 13:2
The beast I saw resembled a leopard, but had feet like those of a bear and a mouth like that of a lion. The dragon gave the beast his power and his throne and great authority.

Isaiah 11:6
The wolf will live with the lamb, the leopard will lie down with the goat, the calf and the lion and the yearling [a] together; and a little child will lead them.

LEPROSY
Is a sign of sin.

LIFT
As we know lifting is rising but it has another spiritual meaning depending on the dream, revelation or vision.

LIFT UP ONE'S FACE IN THE PRESENCE OF ANOTHER
Is a sign of appearing BOLDLY in his presence.

2 SAMUEL 2:22
Again Abner warned Asahel, "Stop chasing me! Why should I strike you down? How could I look your brother Joab in the face?"

EZRA 9:6
and prayed: "I am too ashamed and disgraced, my God, to lift up my face to you, because our sins are higher than our heads and our guilt has reached to the heavens.

LIFTING OF HANDS
Means taking an oath.

GENESIS 14:22
But Abram said to the king of Sodom, "With raised hand I have sworn an oath to the LORD, God Most High, Creator of heaven and earth.

EXODUS 6:8
And I will bring you to the land I swore with uplifted hand to give to Abraham, to Isaac and to Jacob. I will give it to you as a possession. I am the LORD.' "

LIFTING HANDS AGAINST SOMEONE
Is a sign of attacking to fight the person.

2 SAMUEL 18:28
Then Ahimaaz called out to the king, "All is well!" He bowed down before the king with his face to the ground and said, "Praise be to the LORD your God! He has delivered up those who lifted their hands against my lord the king.

LIGHT
Is the expression of God himself

1 JOHN 1:5
This is the message we have heard from him and declare to you: God is light; in him there is no darkness at all.

JOHN 1:5
The light shines in the darkness, and the darkness has not overcome it.

JAMES 1:17
Every good and perfect gift is from above, coming down from the Father of the heavenly lights, who does not change like shifting shadows.

LIGHTENING
Is a symbol of God's glory and awesome majesty.

REVELATION 4:5
From the throne came flashes of lightning, rumblings and peals of thunder. Before the throne, seven lamps were blazing. These are the seven spirits of God.

LINE
Means precepts and rules.

Isaiah 28:10-13
10 *For it is: Do this, do that, a rule for this, a rule for that [a]; a little here, a little there."*
11 *Very well then, with foreign lips and strange tongues God will speak to this people,12 to whom he said, "This is the resting place, let the weary rest"; and, "This is the place of repose"- but they would not listen.*
13 *So then, the word of the LORD to them will become: Do this, do that, a rule for this, a*

rule for that; a little here, a little there- so that as they go they will fall backward; they will be injured and snared and captured

LION
Royal attribute of Christ - Strength

REVELATION 5:5
Then one of the elders said to me, Stop weeping! See, the lion of the tribe of Judah, the root of David, has won! He can open the scroll and break its seven seals!

LION TEETH
Wild beast devastated
It is also a symbol of the cruelty and rapacity of the wicked.

DEUTERONOMY 32:24
I will send wasting famine against them, consuming pestilence and deadly plague; I will send against them the fangs of wild beasts, the venom of vipers that glide in the dust.

JOB 4:10
The lions may roar and growl, yet the teeth of the great lions are broken.

LOCUST
Meaning - Destructive enemies

JOEL 1:4-7
4 *What the locust swarm has left the great locusts have eaten; what the great locusts have left the young locusts have eaten; what the young locusts have left other locusts have eaten.*
5 *Wake up, you drunkards and weep! Wail, all you drinkers of wine; wail because of the new wine, for it has been snatched from your lips.*
6 *A nation has invaded my land, a mighty army without number; it has the teeth of a lion, the fangs of a lioness. 7 It has laid waste my vines and ruined my fig trees. It has stripped off their bark and thrown it away, leaving their branches white.*

M

MARRIAGE
Is a sign of a covenant or relationship

ISAIAH 54:5
For your Maker is your husband- the LORD Almighty is his name- the Holy One of Israel is your Redeemer; he is called the God of all the earth.

ISAIAH 62:4-5
4 *No longer will they call you Deserted, or name your land Desolate. But you will be called Hephzibah, and your land Beulah; for the LORD will take delight in you, and your land will be married.*
5 *As a young man marries a young woman, so will your Builder marry you; as a bridegroom rejoices over his bride, so will your God rejoice over you.*

REVELATION 22:17
The Spirit and the bride say, "Come!" And let those who hear say, "Come!" Let those who are thirsty come; and let all who wish take the free gift of the water of life.

MOUNTIAN
i) Is symbolic of strength and stability

PSALMS 30:7
LORD, when you favoured me, you made my royal mountain [a] stand firm; but when you hid your face I was dismayed.

ii) It also signifies places or sources of strength.

JEREMIAH 3:23
Surely the [idolatrous] commotion on the hills and mountains is a deception; surely in the LORD our God is the salvation of Israel.

iii) It also means someone in authority.

PSALMS 72:3
May the mountains bring prosperity to the people, the hills the fruit of righteousness.

iv) It signifies difficulties.

ISAIAH 40:4
Every valley shall be raised up, every mountain and hill made low; the rough ground shall become level, the rugged places a plain

M

MOUNTIANS DROPPING NEW WINE

Is a sign of abundance.

AMOS 9:13

"The days are coming," declares the LORD, "when the reaper will be overtaken by the one who plows and the planter by the one treading grapes. New wine will drip from the mountains and flow from all the hills,"

MOUNTIAN LAID WASTE

Symbolises desolation

MALACHI 1:3

but Esau I have hated and I have turned his hill country into a wasteland and left his inheritance to the desert jackals."

MOVEMENT OF THE HANDS

Signifies judgement or punishment.

PSALMS 81:14

How quickly I would subdue their enemies and turn my hand against their foes!

AMOS 1:8

I will destroy the king of Ashdod and the one who holds the scepter in Ashkelon. I will turn my hand against Ekron, till the last of the Philistines are dead," says the Sovereign LORD.

ZECHARIAH 13:7

Awake, sword, against my shepherd, against the man who is close to me!" declares the LORD Almighty. "Strike scattered, and I will turn my hand against the little ones.

N

NAKEDNESS
Stripe off glory, power, resources, defence and protection

i) Also signifies destruction

JEREMIAH 49:10
But I will strip Esau bare; I will uncover his hiding places, so that he cannot conceal himself. His armed men are destroyed, also his allies and neighbours, so there is no one to say,

ii) Also means weak and ruined part of a nation which is exposed to danger.

GENESIS 42:9
Then he remembered his dreams about them and said to them, "You are spies! You have come to see where our land is unprotected."

iii) Is also a manifestation of destruction.

JOB 26:6
Death is naked before God; Destruction lies uncovered.

HEBREW 4:13
Nothing in all creation is hidden from God's sight. Everything is uncovered and laid bare before the eyes of him to whom we must give account.

iv) Also symbolises stripping off righteousness through idolatry

EZEKIEL 16:36-39
36 *This is what the Sovereign LORD says: Because you poured out your lust and exposed your nakedness in your promiscuity with your lovers, and because of all your detestable idols, and because you gave them your children's blood,*
37 *therefore I am going to gather all your lovers, with whom you found pleasure, those you loved as well as those you hated. I will gather them against you from all around and will strip you in front of them, and they will see all your nakedness.*
38 *I will sentence you to the punishment of women who commit adultery and who shed blood; I will bring on you the blood vengeance of my wrath and jealous anger.*
39 *Then I will deliver you into the hands of your lovers, and they will tear down your mounds and destroy your lofty shrines. They will strip you of your clothes and take your fine jewellery and leave you naked and bare.*

N

NET
Signifies traps and therefore, we shall look at the following areas of significance.

NET SPREADING
Is an image of subtle devices of the enemy

PSALMS 9:15
The nations have fallen into the pit they have dug; their feet are caught in the net they have hidden.

PSALMS 10:9, 16
Like a lion in cover they lie in wait. They lie in wait to catch the helpless and drag them off in their net all of them up with hooks , he catches them in his net t, he gathers them up in his dragnet; and so he rejoices and is glad

O

OSTRICH
Extreme desolation in the desert.

JOB 30:29
I have become a brother of jackals, a companion of owls.

OX GOES TO THE SLAUGHTER
A rushing youth

OX LICKING GRASS
Meaning - Easy Victory

OWL
This particular bird operates at night and lives in desert places only. So seeing this in a dream or vision, God is literally letting you know how hard, wickedness of highest hierarchy of darkness is standing against you.
This is a symbol of high intensity of spiritual wickedness from the dark world, bringing, disasters, lack and dryness.

OX - ROAMING
A sign of liberation

P

PALM BRANCHES
Symbol of victory

REVELATION 7:9
After this I looked and a vast host appeared which no one could count of every nation, from all tribes and peoples and languages. These stood before the throne and before the lamb; they were attired in white robes, with palm branches in their hands.

PALM TREES
Fruitful people enjoying their prosperity

PSALMS 92:12
The righteous will flourish like a palm tree, they will grow like a cedar of Lebanon;

PEG (TO HOLD TENTS ETC)
National ruler

ZECHARIAH 10:4
From Judah will come the cornerstone, from him the tent peg, from him the battle bow, from him every ruler.

PLOWING A LAND
Is a symbol of repentance

JEREMIAH 4:3
This is what the LORD says to the people of Judah and to Jerusalem: "Break up your unplowed ground and do not sow among thorns.

ISAIAH 2:4
He will judge between the nations and will settle disputes for many peoples. They will beat their swords into plowshares and their spears into pruning hooks. Nation will not take up sword against nation, nor will they train for war anymore.

MALACHI 4:3
Then you will trample on the wicked; they will be ashes under the soles of your feet on the day when I act," says the LORD Almighty.

PLOWING BEHIND SOMEONE
Symbolises scourging

PSALMS 129:3
Ploughmen have ploughed my back and made their furrows long.

PLOWING WITH SOMEONE'S HIEFER
Is a sign of taking unfair advantage of another .

JUDGES 14:18
Before sunset on the seventh day the men of the town said to him,

"What is sweeter than honey? What is stronger than a lion?" Samson said to them, "If you had not plowed with my heifer, you would not have solved my riddle."

POURING WATER ON ANOTHER PERSON'S HAND
Signifies serving that person.

2 KINGS 3:11
But Jehoshaphat asked, "Is there no prophet of the LORD here, through whom we may inquire of the LORD?" An officer of the king of Israel answered, "Elisha son of Shaphat is here. He used to pour water on the hands of Elijah

PRECIOUS STONES
Is a sign of durability and value.

ISAIAH 54:11-12
11 *"Afflicted city, lashed by storms and not comforted, I will rebuild you with stones of turquoise, your foundations with lapis lazuli.*
12 *I will make your battlements of rubies, your gates of sparkling jewels, and all your walls of precious stones.*

REVELATION 4:3
And the one who sat there had the appearance of jasper and ruby. A rainbow that shone like an emerald encircled the throne.

REVELATION 21:11 &21
11 *It shone with the glory of God, and its brilliance was like that of a very precious jewel, like jasper, clear as crystal.*

21 *The twelve gates were twelve pearls, each gate made of a single pearl. The great street of the city was of gold, as pure as transparent glass.*

PRISON
i) Is a symbol of affliction, or bondage to sin / satan.

PSALMS 142:
Set me free from my prison, that I may praise your name. Then the righteous will gather about me because of your goodness to me

ISAIAH 42:7
to open eyes that are blind, to free captives from prison and to release from the dungeon those who sit in darkness.

ISAIAH 61:1
The Spirit of the Sovereign LORD is on me, because the LORD has anointed me to proclaim good news to the poor. He has sent me to bind up the broken hearted, to proclaim

freedom for the captives and release from darkness for the prisoners,

ii) It also means hell

REVELATION 20:7
When the thousand years are over, Satan will be released from his prison

PROSTITUTE OR HARLOT
Is a sign of idolatry

ISAIAH 1:21
See how the faithful city has become a prostitute! She once was full of justice; righteousness used to dwell in her - but now murderers!

JEREMIAH 2:20
Long ago you broke off your yoke and tore off your bonds; you said, 'I will not serve you!' Indeed, on every high hill and under every spreading tree you lay down as a prostitute.

PURE HANDS
Pure action of a person

PRETTY HEIFER
Is a symbol of beauty and wealth

JEREMIAH 46:20
Egypt is a beautiful heifer, but a gadfly is coming against her from the north.

PRIEST'S RIGHT THUMB IN LAMB'S BLOOD
Is a sign of deliverance or consecration by the blood of the lamb or it signifies the blood of Jesus as a seal.

EXODUS 29:20
Slaughter it , take some of its blood and put it on the lobes of the right ears of Aaron and his sons, on the thumbs of their right hands , and on the big toes of the right feet. Then sprinkle blood against the altar on all sides.

LEVITICUS 8:23-24
23 *Moses slaughtered the ram and took some of its blood and put it on the lobe of Aaron's right ear, on the thumb of his right hand and on the big toe of his right foot.*
24 *Moses also brought Aaron's sons forward and put some of the blood on the lobes of their right ears, on the thumbs of their right hands and on the big toes of their right feet. Then he splashed blood against the sides of the altar.*

R

RAIN
Is the word of God.

ISAIAH 55:10
As the rain and the snow come down from heaven, and do not return to it without watering the earth and making it bud and flourish, so that it yields seed for the sower and bread for the eater,

RAIN IN HARVEST - UNTIMELY
Is a symbol of honour given to a fool

PROVERBS 26:1
Like snow in summer or rain in harvest, honour is not fitting for a fool.

RAINBOW
Is a sign of peace between God and man.
It also means a covenant established
It is also a symbol of hope
It symbolises mercy and the love of God.

REVELATION 4:3
And the one who sat there had the appearance of jasper and ruby. A rainbow that shone like an emerald encircled the throne.

RAM / LAMB
Meaning - King of righteousness

LEVITICUS 4:32
'If they bring a lamb as their sin offering, they are to bring a female without defect.

NUMBERS 6:4
As long as they remain under their Nazirite vow, they must not eat anything that comes from the grapevine, not even the seeds or skins.

RAPID FLOWING WATER
Represents the carrier of the wicked.

JOB 24:18
Yet they are foam on the surface of the water; their portion of the land is cursed, so that no one goes to the vineyards.

REAPING A HARVEST
This has many illustrations and is figurative.

i) It is a reward of the wicked.

GALATIANS 6:8
Those who sow to please their sinful nature, from that nature will reap destruction; those who sow to please the Spirit, from the Spirit will reap eternal life.

ii) It also means a reward of righteousness.

HOSEA 10:12
Sow for yourselves righteousness, reap the fruit of unfailing love, and break up your unplowed ground; for it is time to seek the LORD, until he comes and showers his righteousness on you.

iii)It also means temporal support of ministers for spiritual labour.

1 CORINTHIANS 9:11
If we have sown spiritual seed among you, is it too much if we reap a material harvest from you?

iv) It also means final judgement.

MATTHEW13:30-39
30 *Let both grow together until the harvest. At that time I will tell the harvesters: First collect the weeds and tie them in bundles to be burned; then gather the wheat and bring it into my barn."'*
31 *He told them another parable: "The kingdom of heaven is like a mustard seed, which a man took and planted in his field.*
32 *Though it is the smallest of all seeds, yet when it grows, it is* the largest of garden plants and becomes a tree, so that the birds come and perch in its branches.
33 *He told them still another parable: "The kingdom of heaven is like yeast that a woman took and mixed into about sixty pounds of flour until it worked all through the dough.*
34 *Jesus spoke all these things to the crowd in parables; he did not say anything to them without using a parable.*
35 *So was fulfilled what was spoken through the prophet: "I will open my mouth in parables, I will utter things hidden since the creation of the world."*
36 *Then he left the crowd and went into the house. His disciples came to him and said, "Explain to us the parable of the weeds in the field."*
37 *He answered, "The one who sowed the good seed is the Son of Man.*
38 *The field is the world, and the good seed stands for the people of the kingdom. The weeds are the people of the evil one,*
39 *and the enemy who sows them is the devil. The harvest is the end of the age, and the harvesters are angels.*

v) It also means that the ploughman will over take the reaper.

Amos 9:13
The days are coming," declares the LORD, "when the reaper will be overtaken by the one who plows and the planter by the one treading grapes. New wine will drip from the mountains and flow from all the hills,

vi) It also means abundant and continuous harvest.

LEVITICUS 26:5
Your threshing will continue until grape harvest and the grape harvest will continue until planting, and you will eat all the food you want and live in safety in your land.

REED SHAKEN BY THE WIND
**Symbolises a fickle person.
It also symbolises spiritual misery and helplessness.**

MATTHEW 11:7
As John's disciples were leaving, Jesus began to speak to the crowd about John: "What did you go out into the wilderness to see? A reed swayed by the wind?

REPTILES
Unclean things.

RIGHT HAND POINTING A DIRECTION
Indicates - Southward.

1 SAMUEL 23:19
The Ziphites went up to Saul at Gibeah and said, "Is not David hiding among us in the strongholds at Horesh, on the hill of Hakilah, south of Jeshimon?

RIGHT HAND SIDE
Represents a place of honour.

1 KINGS 2:19
When Bathsheba went to King Solomon to speak to him for Adonijah, the king stood up to meet her, bowed down to her and sat down on his throne. He had a throne brought for the king's mother, and she sat down at his right hand.

MARK 14:62
"I am," said Jesus. "And you will see the Son of Man sitting at the right hand of the Mighty One and coming on the clouds of heaven."

R

RING IN A PIG'S NOSE
Is a beautiful woman without discretion.

PROVERBS 11:22
Like a gold ring in a pig's snout is a beautiful woman who shows no discretion.

ROD
Is a sign of discipline.

PROVERBS 13:24
Those who spare the rod hate their children, but those who love them are careful to discipline them.

ROOF
When someone is under it, is a sign of hospitality.

Genesis 19:8
Look, I have two daughters who have never slept with a man. Let me bring them out to you, and you can do what you like with them. But don't do anything to these men, for they have come under the protection of my roof.

MATTHEW 8:8
The centurion replied, "Lord, I do not deserve to have you come under my roof. But just say the word, and my servant will be healed.

ROOM
Is a sense of opening or entrance to opportunities.

PROVERBS 18:16
A man's gift makes room for him and brings him before great men.

ROOT
Is a symbol of strong established foundation and origin or essential cause of everything.

1 TIMOTHY 6:10
For the love of money is a root of all kinds of evil. Some people, eager for money, have wandered from the faith and pierced themselves with many griefs.

EPHESIANS 3:17
So that Christ may dwell in your hearts through faith. And I pray that you, being rooted and established in love,

ROOT DRIED UP
Symbol of loss of vitality.

HOSEA 9:16
Ephraim is blighted, their root is withered, they yield no fruit. Even if they bear children, I will slay their cherished offspring."

R

ROOT OF A PLANT NEAR WATER
Is a sign of prosperity

JOB 29:19
My roots will reach to the water, and the dew will lie all night on my branches.

ROOT OPEN TO WATER
Means no lack.

EZEKIEL 31:7
It was majestic in beauty, with its spreading boughs, for its roots went down to abundant waters.

ROOT EXPOSED
Means - uproot, destroy or remove

LUKE 17:6
He replied, "If you have faith as small as a mustard seed, you can say to this mulberry tree, 'Be uprooted and planted in the sea,' and it will obey you.

RUIN
Is a sign of downfall

EZEKIEL 18:30
"Therefore, house of Israel, I will judge each of you according to your own ways, declares the Sovereign LORD. Repent! Turn away from all your offences; then sin will not be your downfall.

SACRIFICING A NET
Means that someone has employed honour due to God.

HABAKKUK 1:16
Therefore he sacrifices to his net and burns incense to his dragnet, for by his net he lives in luxury and enjoys the choicest food.

SALT
Preservation
Means hospitality
It also signifies grace in heart.

MATTHEW 5:13
"You are the salt of the earth. But if the salt loses its saltiness, how can it be made salty again? It is no longer good for anything, except to be thrown out and trampled underfoot.

SALTED WITH FIRE
Means purification of the good and punishment of sinners.

MARK 9:49
Everyone will be salted with fire.

SAND
Means stability

PROVERBS 27:3
Stone is heavy and sand a burden, but a fool's provocation is heavier than both.

Shifting sand means instability

MATTHEW 7:26
But everyone who hears these words of mine and does not put them into practice is like a foolish man who built his house on sand

SCATTERING OF ASHES
Represents perishability and worthlessness.

GENESIS 18:27
Then Abraham spoke up again: "Now that I have been so bold as to speak to the Lord, though I am nothing but dust and ashes

SCEPTER
Signifies supreme power.

GENESIS 49:10
The scepter will not depart from Judah, nor the ruler's staff from between his feet, until he to whom it belongs shall come and the obedience of the nations be his.

NUMBERS 24:17
I see him, but not now; I behold him, but not near. A star will come out of Jacob; a scepter will rise out of Israel. He will crush the foreheads of Moab, the skulls of all the people of Sheth.

SCOURGE OR BEATEN OR FLOGGING

Is a symbol of lash of the tongue or wordy strife.

PSALMS 31:20

In the shelter of your presence you hide them from all human intrigues; you keep them safe in your dwelling from accusing tongues.

HEBREWS 12:6

Because the Lord disciplines those he loves, and he chastens everyone he accepts as his child."

SEA

Has different figurative so I will explain from different places or occurrences where man stands.

SEA IN ABUNDANCE

Means everything of value is possessed by those in authority such as merchants, businesses, employments etc.

ISAIAH 60:5

Then you will look and be radiant, your heart will throb and swell with joy; the wealth on the seas will be brought to you, to you the riches of the nations will come.

EZEKIEL 26:16

Then all the princes of the coast will step down from their thrones and lay aside their robes and take off their embroidered garments. Clothed with terror, they will sit on the ground, trembling every moment, appalled at you.

SEA ROARING

Is a noise of hostile armies.

SEA SPEAKING

Is a sign of lamenting.

SEA WAVES

i) Represents RIGHTEOUSNESS

ISAIAH 48:18

If only you had paid attention to my commands, your peace would have been like a river, your well-being like the waves of the sea.

ii) Also represents a devastating army

EZEKIEL 26:3-4

3 *Therefore this is what the Sovereign LORD says: I am against you, Tyre, and I will bring many nations against you, like the sea casting up its waves.*

4 *They will destroy the walls of Tyre and pull down her towers; I will scrape away her rubble and make her a bare rock.*

iii)Represents restlessness of the wicked

ISAIAH 57:20
But the wicked are like the tossing sea, which cannot rest, whose waves cast up mire and mud.

iv)Also represents unsteadiness.

JAMES 1:16
Don't be deceived, my dear brothers and sisters.

SEA TO SEA
Means from one place to another or from one end to another

AMOS 8:12
People will stagger from sea to sea and wander from north to east, searching for the word of the LORD, but they will not find it.

MICAH 7:12
In that day people will come to you from Assyria and the cities of Egypt, even from Egypt to the Euphrates and from sea to sea and from mountain to mountain.

SEA WITH DOORS
Means restraining.

JOB 38:8
"Who shut up the sea behind doors when it burst forth from the womb,

SEAL OR SIGNET RING OF A KING
Represents many things as well depending on the situation, condition or time.

I will elaborate with few examples and symbols.

SEAL
Is a sign of ownership.

JOB 9:7
He speaks to the sun and it does not shine; he seals off the light of the stars.

JOB 37:7
So that everyone he has made may know his work, he stops all mortals from their labour.

SEAL
i) Means confirmation.

JEREMIAH 22:24
"As surely as I live," declares the LORD, "even if you, Jehoiachin son of Jehoiakim king of Judah, were a signet ring on my right hand, I would still pull you off.

ISAIAH 8:16
Bind up this testimony of warning and seal up God's instruction among my disciples.

ii) Means something is impenetrable to men but known to Christ's approval.

DANIEL 12:4 & 9
4 But you, Daniel, close up and seal the words of the scroll until the time of the end. Many will go here and there to increase knowledge."

9 He replied, "Go your way, Daniel, because the words are closed up and sealed until the time of the end.

REVELATION 5:2
And I saw a mighty angel proclaiming in a loud voice, "Who is worthy to break the seals and open the scroll?"

SEAL ON SOMETHING
Represents ownership by a higher authority or supreme power

2 TIMOTHY 2:19
Nevertheless, God's solid foundation stands firm, sealed with this inscription: "The Lord knows those who are his," and, "Everyone who confesses the name of the Lord must turn away from wickedness."*

SEALS
Mean permanent establishment.

HAGGAI 2:23
'On that day,' declares the LORD Almighty, 'I will take you, my servant Zerubbabel son of Shealtiel,' declares the LORD, 'and I will make you like my signet ring, for I have chosen you,' declares the LORD Almighty."

SEAT
A dwelling place of authority.

JOB 23:3
If only I knew where to find him; if only I could go to his dwelling!

SEED
i) Is a symbol of posterity of man or future life

GENESIS 3:15
And I will put enmity between you and the woman, and between your offspring and hers; he will crush your head, and you will strike his heel."

GENESIS 4:25
Adam made love to his wife again, and she gave birth to a son and named him Seth, saying,

"God has granted me another child in place of Abel, since Cain killed him."

ii) Means offspring of man.

ROMANS 4:16
Therefore, the promise comes by faith, so that it may be by grace and may be guaranteed to all Abraham's offspring-not only to those who are of the law but also to those who have the faith of Abraham. He is the father of us all.

iii)Is figurative of the word of God.

LUKE 8:5
"A farmer went out to sow his seed."

SERPENTS
Is a symbol of temptations - Satanic, deception, and enemy.

MATTHEW 23:33
"You snakes! You brood of vipers! How will you escape being condemned to hell?

ISAIAH 14:29
Do not rejoice, all you Philistines, that the rod that struck you is broken; from the root of that snake will spring up a viper, its fruit will be a darting, venomous serpent.

JEREMIAH 8:17
See, I will send venomous snakes among you, vipers that cannot be charmed, and they will bite you," declares the LORD.

PSALMS 58:4
Their venom is like the venom of a snake, like that of a cobra that has stopped its ears,

PROVERBS 3:31-32
31 *Do not envy the violent or choose any of their ways.*
32 *For the LORD detests the perverse but takes the upright into his confidence.*

ECCLESIASTES 10:8
Whoever digs a pit may fall into it; whoever breaks through a wall may be bitten by a snake.

MARK 16:18
"they will pick up snakes with their hands; and when they drink deadly poison, it will not hurt them at all; they will place their hands on sick people, and they will get well."

SETTING A TABLE WITH BLEMISHED FOOD
Is a figure of feigned (pretentious) friendship, eating especially in the presence of enemies.

S

PSALMS 23:5
You prepare a table before me in the presence of my enemies. You anoint my head with oil; my cup overflows.

ISAIAH 21:5
They set the tables, they spread the rugs, they eat, they drink! Get up, you officers, oil the shields!

SHADOW
i) **Deep shadow - Is a shadow of death, taking from darkness, gloom and of grave.**

JOB 10:21
before I go to the place of no return, to the land of gloom and utter darkness,

JOB 12:22
He reveals the deep things of darkness and brings utter darkness into the light.

JOB 16:16
My face is red with weeping, dark shadows ring my eyes;
ii) **It also means severe trial in a state of ignorance**

PSALMS 23:4
Even though I walk through the darkest valley, [a] I will fear no evil, for you are with me; your rod and your staff, they comfort me.

MATTHEW 4:16
the people living in darkness have seen a great light; on those living in the land of the shadow of death a light has dawned."

iii) **A shadow swiftly moving is symbolic of the fleetness of human life.**

1 CHRONICLES 29:5
for the gold work and the silver work, and for all the work to be done by the skilled workers. Now, who among you is willing to consecrate yourself to the LORD today?"

JOB 8:9
For we were born only yesterday and know nothing, and our days on earth are but a shadow.

SHARP TEETH BREAKING THINGS
Is a sign of oppression

PROVERBS 30:14
those whose teeth are swords and whose jaws are set with knives to devour the poor from the earth and the needy from among humankind.

S

SHEEP
Is an emblem of meekness, submission and patience.

ISAIAH 53:7
He was oppressed and afflicted, yet he did not open his mouth; he was led like a lamb to the slaughter, and as a sheep before its shearers is silent, so he did not open his mouth.

ACTS 8:32
This is the passage of Scripture the eunuch was reading: "He was led like a sheep to the slaughter and as a lamb before its shearer is silent, so he did not open his mouth.

SHIELD
Means God's protection

GENESIS 15:1
After this, the word of the LORD came to Abram in a vision: "Do not be afraid, Abram. I am your shield, your very great reward.

SHIP WRECK
Departing from the faith

1 TIMOTHY 1:19
holding on to faith and a good conscience, which some have rejected and so have suffered shipwreck with regard to the faith.

SINGING MOUNTAINS
Is a sign of great joy

ISAIAH 44:23
Sing for joy, you heavens, for the LORD has done this; shout aloud, you earth beneath. Burst into song, you mountains, you forests and all your trees, for the LORD has redeemed Jacob, he displays his glory in Israel.

ISAIAH 55:12
You will go out in joy and be led forth in peace; the mountains and hills will burst into song before you, and all the trees of the field will clap their hands.

SIT ON A THRONE
Means exercising legal power

DEUTERONOMY 17:18
When he takes the throne of his kingdom, he is to write for himself on a scroll a copy of this law, taken from that of the Levitical priests.

1 KINGS 16:11
As soon as he began to reign and was seated on the throne, he killed off Baasha's whole family. He did not spare a single male, whether relative or friend.

S

SITTING ROUND A TABLE
Also denotes a sense of security

PSALMS 23:5
You prepare a table before me in the presence of my enemies. You anoint my head with oil; my cup overflows.

SKIN
When you see two skins or a skin from a skin - means giving up one's skin to preserve the other.
Is a prototype of characters of a personality.

JOEL 2:4
They have the appearance of horses; they gallop along like cavalry.

JEREMIAH 13:23
Can an Ethiopian change his skin or a leopard its spots? Neither can you do good who are accustomed to doing evil.

SKIRT OR GARMENT OF A WOMAN BEING RAISED.
Is a sign or symbol of insult and disgrace.

JEREMIAH 13:22 & 26
And if you ask yourself, "Why has this happened to me?"- it is because of your many sins that your skirts have been torn off and your body mistreated. 26 I will pull up your skirts over your face that your shame may be seen

NAHUM 3:5
I am against you," declares the LORD Almighty. "I will lift your skirts over your face. I will show the nations your nakedness and the kingdoms your shame.

SKY
Is a figurative of an expression to denote omnipotence of God - All power

DEUTERONOMY 33:26
"There is no one like the God of Jeshurun, who rides on the heavens to help you and on the clouds in his majesty.

SLEEP
i) **It has many meanings, it is resting the body.**
ii) **It also means moral slackness indolence or stupid activities of the wicked**

ROMANS 13:11-12
11 *And do this, understanding the present time. The hour has already come for you to wake up from your slumber, because our salvation is nearer now than when we first believed.*

12 *The night is nearly over; the day is almost here. So let us put aside the deeds of darkness and put on the armour of light.*

iii) It is a symbol of death.
DANIEL 12:2
Multitudes who sleep in the dust of the earth will awake: some to everlasting life, others to shame and everlasting contempt.

JOHN 11:11
After he had said this, he went on to tell them, "Our friend Lazarus has fallen asleep; but I am going there to wake him up."

SNOW
Also means cleansing power, brilliance and purity.

i) Brilliance
DANIEL 7:9
As I looked," thrones were set in place, and the Ancient of Days took his seat. His clothing was as white as snow; the hair of his head was white like wool. His throne was flaming with fire, and its wheels were all ablaze.

ii) Purity
MATTHEW 28:3
His appearance was like lightning, and his clothes were white as snow.

REVELATION 1:14
The hair on his head was white like wool, as white as snow, and his eyes were like blazing fire.

iii) Cleansing power.

ISAIAH 1:18
Come now, let us reason together," says the LORD. "Though your sins are like scarlet, they shall be as white as snow; though they are red as crimson, they shall be like wool.

LAMENTATIONS 4:7
Their princes were brighter than snow and whiter than milk, their bodies more ruddy than rubies, their appearance like lapis lazuli.

JOB 9:30
Even if I washed myself with soap and my hands with cleansing powder,

EXODUS 4:6
Then the LORD said, "Put your hand inside your cloak." So Moses put his hand into his cloak, and when he took it out, the skin was leprous - it had become as white as snow.

SNOW FERTILIZING THE EARTH BEFORE TURNING TO VAPOUR INTO THE SKY
Is the effective power of God's word.

ISAIAH 55:10
As the rain and the snow come down from heaven, and do not return to it without watering the earth and making it bud and flourish, so that it yields seed for the sower and bread for the eater,

SNOW MELTED AND EASILY DRIED UP IN THE BURNING SUN
Is an expression of the swift and utter destruction of the godless people.

JOB 24: 19
Drought and heat consume the snow waters; so does Sheol (the place of the dead) those who have sinned.

SOMEONE POINTING AND STANDING ON YOUR RIGHT HAND
Symbol of an accuser - to accuse you in trial.

PSALMS 109:6
Appoint someone evil to oppose my enemy; let an accuser stand at his right hand. Zechariah 3:1 Then he showed me Joshua the high priest standing before the angel of the LORD, and Satan standing at his right side to accuse him.

SOMETHING BEING REFINED
Is corrective judgement of God It also means purity of God's word.

ISAIAH 1:25
I will turn my hand against you; I will thoroughly purge away your dross and remove all your impurities.

ISAIAH 48:10
See, I have refined you, though not as silver; I have tested you in the furnace of affliction.

ZECHARIAH 13:9
This third I will bring into the fire; I will refine them like silver and test them like gold. They will call on my name and I will answer them; I will say, 'They are my people,' and they will say, 'The LORD is our God.'

MALACHI 3:2-32
2 But who can endure the day of his coming? Who can stand when he appears? For he will be

S

like a refiner's fire or a launderer's soap.

3 He will sit as a refiner and purifier of silver; he will purify the Levites and refine them like gold and silver. Then the LORD will have men who will bring offerings in righteousness,

SONGS OR SINGING
Is an indication of joy.

ISAIAH 30:29
And you will sing as on the night you celebrate a holy festival; your hearts will rejoice as when people playing pipes go up to the mountain of the LORD, to the Rock of Israel.

SOWING SEED
Is a symbol of scattering or dispersing people

ZECHARIAH 10:9
Though I scatter them among the peoples, yet in distant lands they will remember me. They and their children will survive, and they will return.

1 CORINTHIANS 9:11
If we have sown spiritual seed among you, is it too much if we reap a material harvest from you?

SPIDER
Is the trust of the ungodly and secrets of the wicked.

It also represents the worthless and deceptive character of the wicked.

JOB 8:14
What they trust in is fragile; what they rely on is a spider's web.

SPRINKLING
Generally is sign of conscience purification.

HEBREWS 10:22
Let us draw near to God with a sincere heart in full assurance of faith, having our hearts sprinkled to cleanse us from a guilty conscience and having our bodies washed with pure water.

EXODUS 24:8
Moses then took the blood, sprinkled it on the people and said, "This is the blood of the covenant that the LORD has made with you in accordance with all these words."

LEVITICUS 8:11
He sprinkled some of the oil on the altar seven times, anointing the altar and all its utensils and the basin with its stand, to consecrate them.

SPRINKLING OF PURE WATER

Is an indication of purification from the defilement of the dead. (Spiritual Death)

EZEKIEL 36:25

I will sprinkle clean water on you, and you will be clean; I will cleanse you from all your impurities and from all your idols.

STAFF

Is a symbol of authority for any leader apart from kings

JUDGES 5:14

Some came from Ephraim, whose roots were in Amalek; Benjamin was with the people who followed you. From Makir captains came down, from Zebulun those who bear a commander's staff.

STANDING AT THE RIGHT HAND

Indicates protection

PSALMS 16:8

I keep my eyes always on the LORD. With him at my right hand, I will not be shaken.

STAR

i) Is an expression of an exhorted person or a person to be exhorted

NUMBERS 24:17

"I see him, but not now; I behold him, but not near. A star will come out of Jacob; a scepter will rise out of Israel. He will crush the foreheads of Moab, the skulls of all the people of Sheth.

ii) Also denotes princes, kings, rulers and governors of the earth, nobles etc

DANIEL 8:10

It grew until it reached the host of the heavens, and it threw some of the starry host down to the earth and trampled on them.

REVELATION 6:13

and the stars in the sky fell to earth, as figs drop from a fig tree when shaken by a strong wind.

Revelation 8:10-12

10 *The third angel sounded his trumpet, and a great star, blazing like a torch, fell from the sky on a third of the rivers and on the springs of water-*

11 *the name of the star is Wormwood. A third of the waters turned bitter, and many people died from the waters that had become bitter.*

12 The fourth angel sounded his trumpet, and a third of the sun was struck, a third of the moon, and a third of the stars, so that a third of them turned dark. A third of the day was without light, and also a third of the night.

REVELATION 9:1
The fifth angel sounded his trumpet, and I saw a star that had fallen from the sky to the earth. The star was given the key to the shaft of the Abyss.

REVELATION 12:4
Its tail swept a third of the stars out of the sky and flung them to the earth. The dragon stood in front of the woman who was about to give birth, so that it might devour her child the moment he was born.

STOLEN WATER
Means unlawful pleasures with a strange person.

PROVERBS 9:17
"Stolen water is sweet; food eaten in secret is delicious!"

STONES
Have many meanings and uses, the following will help us to draw out the meanings.

i) Stones Literally mean hardness or insensibility

1 SAMUEL 25:37
Then in the morning, when Nabal was sober, his wife told him all these things, and his heart failed him and he became like a stone.

ii) Also means firmness and strength.

GENESIS 49:24
But his bow remained steady; his strong arms stayed [a] limber, because of the hand of the Mighty One of Jacob, because of the Shepherd, the Rock of Israel,

iii)Also means Christians as living stones.

ZECHARIAH 12:3
On that day, when all the nations of the earth are gathered against her, I will make Jerusalem an immovable rock for all the nations. All who try to move it will injure themselves.

STONES BEING THROWN
Is a sign of spoiling an enemy's field.

STONES IN A SCALE
Is a sign of weighing / your weight has been calculated.

DEUTERONOMY 25:13
Do not have two differing weights in your bag-one heavy, one light.

Proverbs 16:1
Honest scales and balances belong to the LORD; all the weights in the bag are of his making.

STONE IN A SLING AND CATAPULTS
Is an ammunition in your hands.

1 SAMUEL 17:40 & 49
40 *Then he took his staff in his hand, chose five smooth stones from the stream, put them in the pouch of his shepherd's bag and, with his sling in his hand, approached the Philistine.*

49 *Reaching into his bag and taking out a stone, he slung it and struck the Philistine on the forehead. The stone sank into his forehead, and he fell facedown on the ground.*

STONE GATHERING OR CLEARING ON A FIELD
Preparation for cultivation

ISAIAH 5:2
He dug it up and cleared it of stones and planted it with the choicest vines. He built a watchtower in it and cut out a winepress as well. Then he looked for a crop of good grapes, but it yielded only bad fruit.

STONES LINED UP AS A WALL
Is a sign of drawn boundaries.

DEUTERONOMY 19:14
Do not move your neighbour's boundary stone set up by your predecessors in the inheritance you receive in the land the LORD your God is giving you to possess.

STRICKING THE TRUTH
Signifies deep shame or sorrow

JEREMIAH 31:19
After I strayed, I repented; after I came to understand, I beat my breast. I was ashamed and humiliated because I bore the disgrace of my youth.'

EZEKIEL 21:12
Cry out and wail, son of man, for it is against my people; it is against all the princes of Israel. They are thrown to the sword along with my people. Therefore beat your breast

STRIKING AND CLAPPING OF HANDS
Denotes extreme anger.

NUMBERS 24:10
Then Balak's anger burned against Balaam. He struck his hands together and said to him, "I summoned you to curse my enemies, but you have blessed them these three times.

EZEKIEL 21:14 & 17
14 *So then, son of man, prophesy and strike your hands together. Let the sword strike twice, even three times. It is a sword for slaughter- a sword for great slaughter, closing in on them from every side.*

17 *I too will strike my hands together, and my wrath will subside. I the LORD have spoken."*

SITTING ON SOMEONE'S THRONE
Means that you will be that person's successor.

1 KINGS 1:13
Go in to King David and say to him, 'My lord the king, did you not swear to me your servant: "Surely Solomon your son shall be king after me, and he will sit on my throne"? Why then has Adonijah become king?'

SUN
Is a sign of God's favour.

PSALMS 84:11
For the LORD God is a sun and shield; the LORD bestows favour and honour; no good thing does he withhold from those whose walk is blameless.

SUN CLEAR AND BRIGHT
Means the purity of the church, future glory of the saints.

DANIEL 12:3
Those who are wise will shine like the brightness of the heavens, and those who lead many to righteousness, like the stars for ever and ever.

JUDGES 5:31
So may all your enemies perish, LORD! But may all who love you be like the sun when it rises in its strength." Then the land had peace forty years.

SUN DARKENED
Means severe calamities coming down.

EZEKIEL 32:7
When I snuff you out, I will cover the heavens and darken their stars; I will cover the sun with a cloud, and the moon will not give its light.

JOEL 2:10 &31
10 *Before them the earth shakes, the heavens tremble, the sun and moon are darkened, and the stars no longer shine.*

31 *The sun will be turned to darkness and the moon to blood before the coming of the great and dreadful day of the LORD.*

MATTHEW 24:29
"Immediately after the distress of those days" 'the sun will be darkened, and the moon will not give its light; the stars will fall from the sky, and the heavenly bodies will be shaken.

REVELATION 9:2
When he opened the Abyss, smoke rose from it like the smoke from a gigantic furnace. The sun and sky were darkened by the smoke from the Abyss.

SUN GOING DOWN AT NOON
Means premature destruction.

JEREMIAH 15:9
The mother of seven will grow faint and breathe her last. Her sun will set while it is still day; she will be disgraced and humiliated. I will put the survivors to the sword before their enemies, "declares the LORD.

AMOS 8:9
In that day,"declares the Sovereign LORD, "I will make the sun go down at noon and darken the earth in broad daylight.

SUN STANDING STILL
Means perpetual blessings.

ISAIAH 60:20
Your sun will never set again, and your moon will wane no more; the Lord will be your everlasting light, and your days of sorrow will end.

TARES
Is a symbol of evil men

LUKE 3:17
His winnowing fork is in his hand to clear his threshing floor and to gather the wheat into his barn, but he will burn up the chaff with unquenchable fire."

TEETH OF SLANDER, LIARS ETC
Is a sign of spears and arrows.

PSALMS 57:4
I am in the midst of lions; I am forced to dwell among man-eating beasts, whose teeth are spears and arrows, whose tongues are sharp swords.

TO ESCAPE FROM THEIR BITING
Means freedom from the enemy

PSALMS 124:6
Praise be to the LORD, who has not let us be torn by their teeth.

TO SHATTER THEM OR SUCH A PERSON.
Means to disable the arrows and spears of your enemies

PSALMS 58:6
Break the teeth in their mouths, O God; LORD, tear out the fangs of those lions!

THE GREATER LIGHT OF THE SUN
Means the glory of Christ, His coming, the word of God and his supreme ruler ship

ISAIAH 13:10
The stars of heaven and their constellations will not show their light. The rising sun will be darkened and the moon will not give its light.

MATTHEW 7:2
For in the same way you judge others, you will be judged, and with the measure you use, it will be measured to you.

MALACHI 4:2
But for you who revere my name, the sun of righteousness will rise with healing in its rays. And you will go out and frolic like well-fed calves.

REVELATION 1:16
In his right hand he held seven stars, and coming out of his mouth was a sharp, double-edged sword. His face was like the sun shining in all its brilliance.

REVELATION 10:1
Then I saw another mighty angel coming down from heaven. He was robed in a cloud, with a rainbow above his head; his face

was like the sun, and his legs were like fiery pillars.

THRESHED MOUNTAIN
Symbolises a heavy judgement.

ISAIAH 41:15
See, I will make you into a threshing sledge, new and sharp, with many teeth. You will thresh the mountains and crush them, and reduce the hills to chaff.

THIRST
i) Is a moral sense of longing after God.

PSALMS 42:2
My soul thirsts for God, for the living God. When can I go and meet with God?

PSALMS 63:1
You, God, are my God, earnestly I seek you; I thirst for you, my whole being longs for you, in a dry and parched land where there is no water.

ii) Thirst also means longing after criminal indulgence

JEREMIAH 2:25
Do not run until your feet are bare and your throat is·dry. But you said, 'It's no use! I love foreign gods, and I must go after them.'

THIRST CONTINIOUS SATISFACTION
Also means fulfilment of desires.

REVELATION 7:16
'Never again will they hunger; never again will they thirst. The sun will not beat down on them,' nor any scorching heat.

THORN HEDGE
Means corruption

MICAH 7:4
The best of them is like a brier, the most upright worse than a thorn hedge. The day of your watchmen has come, the day God visits you. Now is the time of their confusion.

THORNS
Means the wicked one or wickedness

2 SAMUEL 23:6
But evil men are all to be cast aside like thorns, which are not gathered with the hand.

NAHUM 1:10
They will be entangled among thorns and drunk from their wine; they will be consumed like dry stubble.

T

THORNS AND THISTLES
Means hurt from paganism
It is also a symbol of false prophets

EZEKIEL 28:24
'No longer will the people of Israel have malicious neighbours who are painful briers and sharp thorns. Then they will know that I am the Sovereign LORD.

MATTHEW 7:16
By their fruit you will recognize them. Do people pick grapes from thorn bushes, or figs from thistles?

THORNS IN FIRE
Destruction of the wicked.

PSALMS 118:12
They swarmed around me like bees, but they were consumed as quickly as burning thorns; in the name of the LORD I cut them down.

THRONE
Is a symbol of supreme power and dignity.

GENESIS 41:40
You shall be in charge of my palace, and all my people are to submit to your orders. Only with respect to the throne will I be greater than you."

THRONES
Mean designated earthly celestial beings or arch angels.

COLOSSIANS 1:16
For in him all things were created: things in heaven and on earth, visible and invisible, whether thrones or powers or rulers or authorities; all things have been created through him and for him.

TO BE AT ONE'S FEET
Being at service of another to follow him or receive his instructions

TO BREAK TEETH WITH GRAVEL
Is a sign of a forceful figure

LAMENTATIONS 3:16
He has broken my teeth with gravel; he has trampled me in the dust.

TO COVER A WOMAN WITH A SKIRT
Is a sign of holy matrimony.

RUTH 3:9
"Who are you?" he asked. "I am your servant Ruth," she said. "Spread the corner of your garment over me, since you are a family guardian."

TEETH SHATTERED BY CHEEK SMITTEN
Means to disgrace and disable.

PSALMS 3:7
Arise, LORD! Deliver me, my God! Strike all my enemies on the jaw; break the teeth of the wicked.

LAMENTATIONS 3:30
Let them offer their cheeks to one who would strike them, and let them be filled with disgrace.

TORCH
Is God's guidance

2 SAMUEL 22:29
You, LORD, are my lamp; the LORD turns my darkness into light.

PSALMS 18:28
You, LORD, keep my lamp burning; my God turns my darkness into light.

TOWER
Means something strong.

ISAIAH 23:13
Look at the land of the Babylonians, this people that is now of no account! The Assyrians have made it a place for desert creatures; they raised up their siege towers, they stripped its fortresses bare and turned it into a ruin.

TRANSPORTATION
Means a condition of life or destiny

TREE
Meaning - PEOPLE

PSALMS 1:3
They are like a tree planted by stream of water which yields its fruit in season and whose leaf does not wither- whatever they do prospers.

JEREMIAH 17:7 - 8
7 But blessed are those who trust in the LORD, Whose confidence is in him.
8 They will be like a tree planted by the water that sends out its roots by the stream. It does not fear when heat comes; its leaves are always green. It has no worries in a year of drought and never fails to bear fruit."

T

TREE PLANTED BY THE WATER
Is an emblem of righteousness

JEREMIAH 17:8
They will be like a tree planted by the water that sends out its roots by the stream. It does not fear when heat comes; its leaves are always green. It has no worries in a year of drought and never fails to bear fruit."

TURTLE DOVE
Is a symbol of sacrifices made for peace.

GENESIS 15:9
So the LORD said to him, "Bring me a heifer, a goat and a ram, each three years old, along with a dove and a young pigeon."

U

UNJUST HANDS
Presents injustice

W

WALKING
Is a state and conduct of life.

WALKING IN DARKNESS
Is a symbol of unbelief and being misled by error.

1 JOHN 1:6
If we claim to have fellowship with him and yet walk in the darkness, we lie and do not live out the truth.

WALK IN THE LIGHT
Means to be well informed, holy and happy

I JOHN 1:7
But if we walk in the light, as he is in the light, we have fellowship with one another, and the blood of Jesus, his Son, purifies us from all sin.

WALL
i) A wall is a symbol of salvation

ISAIAH 26:1
In that day this song will be sung in the land of Judah: We have a strong city; God makes salvation its walls and ramparts.

ISAIAH 60:8
Who are these that fly along like clouds, like doves to their nests?

ii) Is a symbol of God's protection

ZECHARIAH 2:5
And I myself will be a wall of fire around it,' declares the LORD, 'and I will be its glory within.'

WAR
Is figurative of death.

ECCLESIASTES 8:8
As no one has power over the wind to contain it, so no one has power over the time of their death. As no one is discharged in time of war, so wickedness will not release those who practice it.

WATER
i) Occasionally for tears.

JEREMIAH 9:1
Oh, that my head were a spring of water and my eyes a fountain of tears! I would weep day and night for the slain of my people.

ii) Figurative of trouble

PSALMS 66:12

You let people ride over our heads; we went through fire and water, but you brought us to a place of abundance.

iii) It also denotes misfortune.

LAMENTATIONS 3:54

The waters closed over my head, and I thought I was about to perish.

PSALMS 69:1

Save me, O God, for the waters have come up to my neck.

iv) Also means persecutions.

PSALMS 88:17

All day long they surround me like a flood; they have completely engulfed me.

v) Also means a hostile army.

ISAIAH 8:7

Therefore the Lord is about to bring against them the mighty floodwaters of the Euphrates the king of Assyria with all his pomp. It will overflow all its channels, run over all its banks.

ISAIAH 17:13

Although the peoples roar like the roar of surging waters, when he rebukes them they flee far away, driven before the wind like chaff on the hills, like tumbleweed before a gale.

v) Also means children or prosperity.

NUMBERS 24:7

Water will flow from their buckets; their seed will have abundant water." Their king will be greater than Agag; their kingdom will be exalted.

ISAIAH 48:1

Listen to this, house of Jacob, you who are called by the name of Israel and come from the line of Judah, you who take oaths in the name of the LORD and invoke the God of Israel- but not in truth or righteousness

vi) It is a symbol of clouds.

PSALMS 104:3

and lays the beams of his upper chambers on their waters. He makes the clouds his chariot and rides on the wings of the wind.

vii)Is a symbol of the refreshing power of the Holy spirit.

ISAIAH 12:3

With joy you will draw water from the wells of salvation.

ISAIAH 35:6-7

6 *Then will the lame leap like a deer, and the mute tongue shout for joy. Water will gush forth in the wilderness and streams in the desert.*

7 *The burning sand will become a pool, the thirsty ground bubbling springs. In the haunts where jackals once lay, grass and reeds and papyrus will grow.*

ISAIAH 55:1

Come, all you who are thirsty, come to the waters; and you who have no money, come, buy and eat! Come, buy wine and milk without money and without cost.

viii) It also a symbol of divine support, the gift and grace of the Holy Spirit.

JOHN 7:37

On the last and greatest day of the Festival, Jesus stood and said in a loud voice," Let anyone who is thirsty come to me and drink.

ISAIAH 44:3

For I will pour water on the thirsty land, and streams on the dry ground; I will pour out my Spirit on your offspring, and my blessing on your descendants.

EZEKIEL 36:2

I will sprinkle clean water on you, and you will be clean; I will cleanse you from all your Impurities and from all your idols.

WATER POURED OUT

Means God's wrath and fainting by terror Termination process.

HOSEA 5:10

Judah's leaders are like those who move boundary stones. I will pour out my wrath on them like a flood of water.

PSALMS 22:14

I am poured out like water, and all my bones are out of joint. My heart has turned to wax; it has melted within me.

1 KINGS 11:26-27

26 *Also, Jeroboam son of Nebat rebelled against the king. He was one of Solomon's officials, an Ephraimite from Zeredah, and his mother was a widow named Zeruah.*

27 *Here is the account of how he rebelled against the king: Solomon had built the terraces and had filled in the gap in the wall of the city of David his father.*

WATER SPILLED ON THE GROUND
Is a figure of death.

2 SAMUEL 14:14
Like water spilled on the ground, which cannot be recovered, so we must die. But God does not take away life; instead, he devises ways so that a banished person may not remain estranged from him.

WATERED GARDEN
A sign of fertility

ISAIAH 58:11
The LORD will guide you always; he will satisfy your needs in a sun-scorched land and will strengthen your frame. You will be like a well-watered garden, like a spring whose waters never fail.

WATERLESS GARDEN
Dryness or a desert which is a sign or scarcity

ISAIAH 1:30
You will be like an oak with fading leaves, like a garden without water.

WELL
Is figurative of God as a source of salvation.

JOHN 4:10
Jesus answered her, "If you knew the gift of God and who it is that asks you for a drink, you would have asked him and he would have given you living water

WAVERING WATERS
Is instability

GENESIS 49:4
Turbulent as the waters, you will no longer excel, for you went up onto your father's bed, onto my couch and defiled it.

WHIRLWIND
Is sweeping destruction sure to overtake the wicked.

PSALMS 58:9
Before your pots can feel the heat of the thorns- whether they be green or dry-the wicked will be swept away.

ISAIAH 41:16
You will winnow them, the wind will pick them up, and a gale will blow them away. But you will rejoice in the LORD and glory in the Holy One of Israel.

WHITE STONES
Is a sign of reward after labour to victory which cannot be tampered with.

REVELATION 2:17
Whoever has ears, let them hear what the Spirit says to the churches. To those who are victorious, I will give some of the hidden manna. I will also give each of them a white stone with a new name written on it, known only to the one who receives it.

WHITE TEETH
Is figurative of abundance and plenty

GENESIS 49:12
His eyes will be darker than wine, his teeth whiter than milk.

WHITE WASHED WALLLS
Is a sign of hypocrisy.

ACTS 23:3
Then Paul said to him, "God will strike you, you whitewashed wall! You sit there to judge me according to the law, yet you yourself violate the law by commanding that I be struck!"

WILD WAVES OF THE SEA
Is a figurative of false teachers or prophets.

JUDE 1:13
They are wild waves of the sea, foaming up their shame;
wandering stars, for whom blackest darkness has been reserved forever.

WINE
Is a symbol of the blood of Christ and the blessings of the gospel

MATTHEW 26:27-29
27 Then he took the cup, gave thanks and offered it to them, saying, "Drink from it, all of you. 28 This is my blood of the covenant, which is poured out for many for the forgiveness of sins. 29 I tell you, I will not drink of this fruit of the vine from now on until that day when I drink it anew with you in my Father's kingdom."

PROVERBS 9:2
She has prepared her meat and mixed her wine: she has also set her table.

WOLF
Is a symbol of the wicked

MATTHEW 10:16
I am sending you out like sheep among wolves. Therefore be as shrewd as snakes and as innocent as doves.

The following understanding of dreams, revelations and visions are extracts from my own deliverance experiences and ministrations of the word of God. God has a greater part to play in our dream world.

BATHING
Is a sign of initiation

GENESIS 10:11
This is my covenant with you and your descendants after you, the covenant you are to keep: Every male among you shall be circumcised.

11 You are to undergo circumcision, and it will be the sign of the covenant between me and you.

JOHN 17:17
Sanctify them by the truth. Your word is truth.

BLOOD
Is a sign of a covenant

GENESIS 17:11
And ye shall circumcise the flesh of your foreskin; and it shall be a token of the covenant between me and you.

MARK 14:24
This is my blood of the covenant, which is poured out for many," he said to them.

BREAST FEEDING
Is releasing productivity to siblings or spiritual children; it may also mean the gift of teaching.

HEBREWS 5:13
Anyone, who lives on milk, being still an infant, is not acquainted with the teaching about righteousness.

1 PETER 2:2
Like newborn babies, crave pure spiritual milk, so that by it you may grow up in your salvation.

BEING IN A STADIUM OR SPORTS GROUND
Is a field of the world

CARRYING BABIES ON THE SEA SIDE OR RIVERSIDE
i) Is spiritual children confiscated by water spirit.

ii) It also means barrenness.

CORN

i) Is a sign of productivity and increase of prosperity

GENESIS **42:2**
He said, "Behold, I have heard that there is grain in Egypt; go down there and buy some for us from that place, so that we may live and not die."

ii) Is a sign of productivity and fruit of the womb.

EATING
Is a sign of witch craft contact point or contamination of the body.

FLYING
Is witch craft in operation

HEARING A WORD
Is a sign of a curse or a blessing depending on what you hear.

PREGNANCY
Is a sign of unfulfilled desires.

RIPE FRUIT
Mature offspring.

SWIMMING
Depending on the act but mostly is contact of water spirits.

SEXUAL INTERCOURSE
Is a marital Covenant and oppression into idolatry.

SEA
Is the world.

SCARLET
Service or sacrifice.

TWO TEAMS PLAYING TOGETHER.
Is a conflict between good and evil.

For more information, counselling and deliverance
kindly contact us on
+44 (0) 208 801 7885,
Fax: **+44 (0) 208 885 4045,**
Email: **drjohn@livingwordtemple.org**
or visit our Website:
www.livingwordtemple.org
for all our other products.

Or visit us at
LIVING WORD TEMPLE
Tottenham Branch
2 Chapel Place, 6 White Hart Lane,
Tottenham, London N17 8DP